MW01001044

How to Really, *Really* Write Those Boring Police Reports!

By Kimberly Clark

Looseleaf Law Publications, Inc.
43-08 162nd Street
Flushing, NY 11358
www.LooseleafLaw.com 800-647-5547

Library of Congress Cataloging-in-Publication Data

Clark, Kimberly, 1965-

How to really, *really* write those boring police reports! / by Kimberly Clark

p. cm.

Includes index.

ISBN 1-889031-41-0

1. Police reports. 2. Report writing. I. Title.

HV7936.R53 C53 2000

808'.066363--dc21

00-047508

Printed in the United States of America

Personal Thanks

Defensive Tactics Super Instructor, and babysitter during construction, Joe.

Legal Beagle, Attorney, Bruce Klienberg

Computer Gurus, Debbie Sinclair and George Seiler

Inspiration, Dad (who kept saying, "Yeah, yeah that looks good")

Editor, Mom (who enjoyed the red penning of my first drafts just a little too much)

Full time babysitter, Angie

Little interrupters, Joseph and Erin

Table of Contents

About the Author iii

Introduction v

Chapter One
Getting Started 1

Chapter Two
Knock on the Door 5

Chapter Three
"Full Report on my Desk in the Morning!" 25

Chapter Four
Grammar and Spelling 55

Chapter Five
Privacy and Legal Issues 67

Chapter Six
Arrest Affidavits 79

Chapter Seven
Use of Force Documentation 91

Chapter Eight
Computer Report Writing 105

Resources 115

About the Author

Kimberly Clark is a 13-year veteran of the Tampa Police Department. She has been a certified instructor of police-related topics since 1990. The topics range from high liability defensive tactics to numerous administrative subjects. Her students include civilian personnel and certified police officers in college academy classes.

Ms. Clark spent several years as a Field Training Officer and continues to teach at the Tampa Police Academy. She also teaches academy classes on-line for the Smith and Wesson Police Academy and is a member of ASLET.

Introduction

Several years ago my police department, located in a major metropolitan city next to an enormous bay, which is world renowned for its shark population, lightning strikes and floating bodies, began a hiring frenzy for police officers. Field Training Officers were badly needed to train the new officers in a 16-week field-training program. The shift was a choice evening shift with a financial incentive and the glowing promise of take home cars and quick promotions to follow for all who became a Trainer.

Since I desperately wanted to leave the midnight shift before I fell asleep driving or lost my ability to see in the daylight I signed up for the Field Trainer class. I completed the course, applied for an FTO position and was assigned to my new squad.

My first new officer was a hulky, husky, quiet natured guy that came from the nearby jail system. He was great. Made my job easy and made me look very good as a new trainer. He knew the importance of never allowing his FTO to get wet or go hungry; his only problem was officer safety.

He was used to being unarmed and in a jail. He was comfortable in any environment and used to standing right next to the bad guy. Occasionally he would carry his flashlight in his weapon hand. After reminding him several times to get that flashlight out of his gun hand, I decided it was time to get serious.

The unconfirmed story goes like this. I cured him of this extremely dangerous habit by first warning him, one more time. He of course forgot again and I apparently reminded him by smacking his bare knuckles that were wrapped around his metal flashlight, with the tip of my own flashlight.

Now, I do not remember this incident ever happening. However, it does sound like something I might do, as a purely corrective measure in safety training, which is paramount for any police officer.

After training several officers that sailed through the program, I was given my first problem officer. His only legitimate difficulty was report writing. Since I had recently been given the honor of teaching report writing, I was the likely candidate to "fix or fire" this new officer.

We began by reviewing his prior written work. It was bad. It was worse than bad, it was horrible. The reports had no organization and created no clear mental picture of the offense. The interviews were scrambled in the investigation area and often repeated the same information twice. He needed special attention and was going to have to work very hard to catch up with the rest of his class.

We began with homework. Our department will not pay overtime to officers that are still in the Field Training Program, so I made it clear to him that he didn't have to complete the homework assignments I was giving him. This gave me the opportunity to see if he was serious about his job and how bad he wanted to continue his training. He came to work the next day with the assignments complete.

We graded them together. He had a grasp of grammar basics and didn't have a problem with the assignments. After several trial reports in a classroom environment with very controlled conditions, we finally went onto the street to take calls and write real police reports. A pattern began to emerge.

This Officer carried three notepads. One in the car for notes from the dispatcher. One in his back pocket for notes he took while talking to his victims. And still another one in his shirt pocket.

When he opened his notepad to write he opened it in the center. He wrote on the front page then flipped the page and wrote on the back of that page. That notepad would go into his pocket. He would walk around, interview someone else and document more information. This was when he removed the second notepad from his shirt pocket and opened it in the center and began the same confusing ritual again.

I watched this with amusement, mentally trying to remember where he was putting all these notes so I could help him retrieve them when the time came to write this report. That time came.

He wanted to go to a sector office so he could spread out all of his notes and write in comfort. I said no.

Training was about to begin!

I let him try to write the report. I watched him as he shuffled through pages and pages of notes. He had failed to label the role of any person he had spoken with and did not know which name in his notes was the victim. He had three notepads he was trying to go through and had them lined up on the dashboard of our car. I let him struggle, all the while noting each situation that would come up and give him a problem. Frustrated, he finally said he needed to go to a sector office, he was used to writing on a desk and he was uncomfortable with just a clipboard to write on.

Welcome to police work.

After an hour of struggling without a pen even being put to paper, I decided to bail him out.

We began with a review of the call. We recited details of the incident; commonly they are given to you out of order. We practiced putting the details back together into chronological order. I made him rewrite all of his notes onto one note pad and throw the other notepads in the trash.

Throughout his training we practiced reviewing calls, saying sentences out loud and organizing his thoughts prior to putting anything on paper.

I sent him out to purchase an automatic speller to carry in his pocket. He was introduced to pen correction fluid, and he was searched every day, prior to our shift, for hidden notepads.

He went from a “fire him or fix him,” to a competent officer that could do the job and write about it.

After several years of experience he is now considered one of the hardest workers in his zone and turns in reports that are considered good, by supervisory standards.

During his training I searched for a book on police report writing to refer to for help. I found many that were very well written. They could show anyone how to write...college level reports that would satisfy the most particular English professor. Of the many books I read, I could not find one that was specific and would get to the point about what was required for documentation of investigations for police work.

As a result of this unsuccessful search and my years of teaching report writing, I developed, redeveloped, fixed and tweaked a method that seems to work very well for my officers. Those years of notes were compiled, along with thoughts and suggestions that came from my students, into written form. I was encouraged, by my husband and my father to put it down on paper permanently by writing a book.

Here goes...

This book is intended to be simple enough for a new officer to use to "hit the street writing," or an experienced officer can use it to refresh. This book is not intended to give your department a whole new way of doing things, just some guidelines to follow to create a solid foundation in your own writing skills.

Be prepared to adapt to departmental and supervisory quirks and requirements for your own agency and expect to learn even more about documenting details and writing skills as your experience grows.

Becoming a police officer is an exciting ride of high-speed car chases, blazing gunfights, writing endless traffic tickets and maybe even delivering the occasional baby. There are lots of exciting moments and, depending on where you work there can be plenty to reminisce about in the parking lot after work or at the local cop bar.

Unlike Hollywood movies and on T.V., where the good guy wanders off into the sunset amid the chaos of scurrying police and firemen, never taking notes or writing a single word…those car chases and gun fights you get into have to be documented by someone. That someone will be you.

Police work is the most rewarding job you can have. It is the most fun you can have legally. But there is always a down side.

Writing police reports is boring. It's not just boring it is tedious, time consuming and sometimes difficult to get started. It has to be completed by the end of your shift. You get to write while relaxing on the police special "clip board desk" wedged into your steering wheel with bad lighting and late hours.

Many people will be reading and scrutinizing your police report. When an incident occurs, there is a victim. Sometimes there will be a bad guy involved. If you catch the bad guy there is even more paperwork. If you are forced to defend yourself or use force on the bad guy to arrest him, it keeps adding up.

Liability concerns will come at you personally and for your agency from every angle.

When you are finally finished with your report and all of its accompanying forms, the report goes to your immediate supervisor for review. After this review you may have a desk supervisor that wants to look at the paperwork that was generated in their zone. This supervisor may make corrections to your report and hand it back to your supervisor for it to be rewritten their way. Once your report finally clears this hurdle it will go to a record keeping section. Most departments will enter the information into a computer database.

At this time most reports become public record. Anyone that wants to pay the copying fee can pick up a copy of the report. If the report gets referred to the detective division for latent investigative work a detective will be reading your report. If a bad guy gets arrested a copy of the report goes to your prosecutor's office for filing charges. The bad guy's attorney, by now, has a copy too. The local media thought this case was of interest and bought a copy also. When you have a deposition, six months later, for the arrest, prior to trial, a copy of the report will be there for you to refresh from. In court the judge has a copy they can read from.

If all went well and you documented all the facts from the investigation and interviews, closed all loopholes and answered all questions that could possibly be asked, you should be fine even under the most grueling cross examination!!!

However, attorneys are paid to do what they do best. They will try to make you look dumb and incompetent on the witness stand in front of a jury, judge, attorneys and anyone else that happens to come into the courtroom. Sometimes a police officer will assist in this process by writing an incomplete report.

There are many documented instances that show what happens when an officer does not write a complete, concise report. Most of these situations are never heard about. Some reports are so incomplete they are given to the Prosecutors Office for filing charges and the arrest is "nolle prosequi." Meaning never filed. Meaning the bad guy had his charges dropped.

Internal affairs will use an officer's report as a document to refer from in complaint cases. If an officer is incomplete in the initial report and is questioned about something, the officer will have an opportunity to explain his actions under oath. However, a later explanation, no matter how innocent the complaint, can make the officer appear to be adding or embellishing to cover up his actions. This can happen in the most simplistic of situations and may make the officer appear untruthful.

All of this can be dramatically improved upon by proper, complete, detailed documentation the first time every time. Your own words you put on paper can help to protect you from civil liability or criminal prosecution, or they cannot.

When you finish this book you will have been given the tools you need to take a call from the radio description, to the crime scene, to paper. You will learn to organize yourself, your notes and your thoughts.

Streamlining your important and relevant facts will be simplified by using a writing formula that is so concise you will feel confident in documenting incidents, even the complex ones, no matter how late in your shift you get started.

Many people you ride with in your training program, and on the street, will have their own style of writing. You will, through time and experience, develop habits you are comfortable with. Be prepared to adapt your style somewhat, to the individual you are working for. Most Sergeants have their own peculiar quirks that must be in every report. Put them in. Some agencies have statements that are necessary for prosecution in your area, add them. This book will give you the basics in good, organized police report writing, however, report writing is subjective.

Being able to adapt an organized format, that includes your incident, appropriate coverage for legal and liability concerns and still is able to add extra's to meet your agencies requirements, is a skill that will be appreciated by everyone. Especially you, when the time comes to read that report months or even years down the road in a crowded courtroom.

On a side note; throughout this book I will refer to a suspect, perpetrator or prisoner as a "bad guy." This is a habit I developed in teaching. My referral keeps bored, semi comatose, half listening students from confusing such terms as "subject" with "suspect" and so on. "Bad guy" is simple, straightforward and every officer in every agency knows what related person I am referring to.

This is not meant to offend anyone. I don't want to take anything away from the other half of the population. I am fully aware that there are "Bad Girls" too. I have seen bad girls do bad things. Some have been just as bad if not badder than the bad guys. This is simply my terminology and my habit, so relax ladies and don't get your polyesters in a wad.

Chapter One
Getting Started

When you complete your academy training and you are at this point you will have read this book, been beat up in defensive tactics and officer survival classes, fired a gun, some for the first time at a paper target. Fallen asleep in some classes and wondered just what you are getting yourself into in some other classes. All of this is perfectly normal!! In Fact, if you are not nervous, apprehensive and downright scared to death on your first call you probably didn't pass the psychological and aren't reading this book anyway.

You're going to be riding with a Field Training Officer for a good portion of your actual street training. You will be in uniform, with a badge and a gun and will have full arrest powers. No one will know you are in training, except those you inform: this will be done unintentionally usually by your own actions. Unfortunately your inexperience will be obvious to those who come into contact with police on a regular basis.

Your uniform will be new, the darkest in color and perfectly pressed, badge will be shiny and so will all your leather gear. This equipment is brand new and will need to be broken in. The bulletproof vest will fit flat as if it just came out of the box and the leather gear will be stiff. Your handcuffs will work smoothly with no signs of dried blood or rust. As a result of this you will fidget and pull at your leather gear and constantly readjust your vest so you can breathe. Your eyes will dart around quickly even on the most mild call and you will have no idea what to do with your hands. All of this will scream rookie!!!!!!!!

First things first...relax. Do not drop your guard ever but learn to become comfortable with all your equipment. Put it on, in full, prior to the start of your first shift. Make surc cverything fits and works, jump up and down a few times and land hard. If anything shifts or comes loose, adjust it, tighten it, bolt it, glue it or do what ever you have to do to secure those items.

In addition to the equipment issued to you, have two black ink pens tucked in your shirt pocket and one single, solitary notepad (in the always accessible and easy to reach, but out of your hands for officer safety purposes rear pants pocket). Some agencies issue fancy notepads with the department logo, some do not. If yours doesn't, go to your nearest office supply store and buy a multi-pac of spiral notepads, 4"X 5" or smaller that fits into your rear pants pocket and does not stick out. If so, it can come out, or become lost in a foot pursuit or a fight.

If spelling is a problem for you, invest in an automatic speller. These useful little gadgets are so small they will fit into your uniform shirt pocket. Find a good quality, pen style correction fluid, AKA: "Rookie Juice," and keep that in your shirt pocket as well.

If you are able, talk to your FTO prior to the start of your shift. Ask them if you will be using their equipment, or if you will need to have all your own equipment. Generally the FTO has their own car, packed with their favorite equipment and you will be using theirs. There is not enough room for two full sets of equipment in one car.

By equipment I mean policy and legal books, report forms, cheat notes, (this book), and rulers for traffic crashes. You will also have items such as tape measures and print kits. A good friend of mine even carries a shovel?! (He says some prisoners just don't make it to booking!!)

What you will need, at an absolute minimum, is a clipboard. Most agencies will issue you a fifty year old aluminum one that is bent in the middle and no longer clips closed. If yours is issued to you in this condition and you cannot get a replacement, buy your own. Law enforcement supply stores carry new, lightweight aluminum clipboards in stock. Look for one that is thick. There is a filing chamber underneath the writing surface that is used for spare reports, extra pens, traffic rulers and an economy size refill of correction fluid. This clipboard does not fit under your car seat but it can be wedged between the seats or over the cage behind your head.

One word of caution here, resist the urge to keep the clipboard on the dash of the car. I have seen more than one clipboard go screaming across the dashboard and right out the window on a fast turn. They always pop open when they hit the ground and the entire written contents of your last few calls goes blowing down the street.

All of the above preparations will make you more comfortable with your equipment and therefore yourself. One very important note.... only carry one notepad at a time. Never carry additional ones in other pockets or a larger one in the car for notes. While you are new and in training you will want to work very hard on developing good safety and investigative habits. Always take a few extra minutes to remain organized and learn to find and use your equipment and reference materials. The goal here is to become self-sufficient as soon as possible while still in the training program.

Chapter Two
Knock on the Door

While en route to your very first call you will probably be the passenger with your FTO. Use this time to silently gape in awe at all the new and confusing toys in the car. Pretend to listen intently to the radio and wear sunglasses in the daytime if you have to hide those darting rookie eyes.!!

Your first call will always be remembered, no matter how mundane. You will be the most polite, attentive and conscientious police officer this complainant has ever encountered. From here on out there will be a rapid downhill slide, as you become a real cop!

When you receive the information about your first call some agencies will have computer dispatch, and some will have voice dispatch by an actual dispatcher. If the call is a voice dispatch offer to write down the information about the call onto your notepad. Document the address, offense, descriptions, and any other details the dispatcher gives you. Confirm the information with your FTO prior to acknowledging the radio. You're on your way!

Usually your FTO will handle this call in its entirety. You can listen without interjecting and practice writing information on your new note pad. Prior to your arrival on the call, think about the offense you are responding to. Remember the criminal elements that must be present for the offense to be complete, or to make an arrest. Make a mental picture of what they are, for example a very common offense reported to police is a burglary.

Some states call this breaking and entering, etc. English Common Law defines a burglary as "the unlawful entry into the nighttime dwelling of another with the intent to commit a felony therein." Many states have expanded this to read, "Entering the structure, conveyance or curtilage of another with the intent to commit a crime." Fortunately this covers almost any time a person enters anything unlawfully, breaking in or walking in an unlocked door and even thinks about committing a crime. For most states burglary must have a secondary crime.

These are the types of details you will look for depending on your particular call or offense.

As you approach your call, look around. Orient yourself to direction, NORTH-SOUTH-EAST-WEST street names, structures, vehicles, bushes and foliage, and anything that may look out of place. Make a mental note of the structure involved or area involved and pay attention to marks on the ground such as torn up grass, skid marks, evidence laying in plain view etc.

Be prepared to take notes of what physical evidence is present at your scene. (More on physical evidence later)

Just in case your FTO throws you to the wolves on the first call, relax pretend you know a little and be friendly.

Begin the conversation with the complainant you come into contact with, with a polite, "Did you call for police?" They will immediately let you know if you have the right person. Dispatch will give you some basic information about this call but you must always confirm every detail with the complainant.

Next ask the complainant, "What happened?" Some complainants are very precise and will get to the point of their call immediately. This is considered the interview portion of your call.

While they are talking, if the conversation begins to ramble, redirect them back to the original complaint with very specific and direct questions. Go over the elements of the state laws individually to make sure they have been met and how they were met. Don't lead your subjects but ask them specific questions and let them answer.

Remember, for some complainants you are their first contact with police. Your job is a complete mystery to them and you will be watched and judged accordingly.

Some of your complainants call police a lot and love the crowd that develops as they state their problem, loudly and with overly expressive body language. There are several techniques you can deploy to calm and control an interview.

One is to remove the complainant from the environment. Take them back into their home if it is safe. Walk them around the corner of the building, or to a distance so bystanders cannot easily hear them, always keeping your partner within sight. Remain alert and always keep your weapon hand empty. Stand in a comfortable interview position.

Have the complainant state the entire problem and go through the details prior to writing down anything or removing that new notepad. If your victim is agitated or upset in any way spend a few extra minutes trying to calm them down. Appear empathetic and allow them to compose themselves. Some of the story and the nature of the problem will have come out by now but it will probably be full of omissions and in need of direct questions by you. Many complainants will have the details of the offense in reverse order of how they actually happened. Details will come to mind as they are speaking and they will give them to you as they remember them. Stop them after every detail and ask where it fit into the picture. Your job will be to reorganize a usually disorganized, disjointed interview from a person that will probably be upset, angry, scared and confused. Doing this takes practice and patience on your part.

By now you will have a basic understanding of your state's criminal laws and will probably even know what type of offense you are dealing with. The easiest way to have a full and complete understanding of how the offense occurred is to have the complainant walk you through.

After the complainant calms down, have them take you back to their exact location when the offense started.

Have the complainant verify the offense did in fact occur on today's date and the approximate time it did happen. Ask the complainant to describe to you the first thing they heard or saw. What was it? What did it sound/look like, where did the noise come from, how far away? Did the complainant see anything just prior to the noise, just after the noise? Who was involved, who was the bad guy (if known) and where is he now, is anyone injured? Is the complainant the victim? Can they positively identify the bad guy and do they wish to prosecute? Most states require this information to continue the investigation and to file the charges for criminal prosecution.

When talking to and listening to your complainant or witness and they give you exact quotes as to what a bad guy said or what they, themselves may have said, note this "in quotations marks." You do not have to do this for everything the complainant says but there are some rules to follow in quoting someone.

If your complainant is the victim of any type of serious crime and the bad guy made a statement to the victim, put that statement in quotes. Bad guys get nervous and some fall into a habit. They might say the same thing over and over to many different victims. Latent investigators will catch onto this after several reports cross their desk, with a robbery suspect telling everyone in the closed restaurant to "Freeze and get into the freezer," and a pattern will eventually emerge.

If a victim is explaining to you how something happened to them and they are using slang or street language that you do not understand, ask for specifics and a definition to make sure everyone is talking about the same act.

Example:

A victim of a sexual battery may say:

Victim: "He skeeted on me!."
Police: Did he ejaculate on you?
Victim: "Yeah, he skeeted on me."

The above example is the victim's language for what happened. It is her language and very specific as to the act that was committed. The word "skeeted" will be in quotations on your report but you will need to translate. A statement immediately following such as...common street term for ejaculation... should be written in the interview. Be prepared to talk at the same level as the victims, in their own language, to conduct your interview and investigation. You will need to "smarten up" the interview when it is put on paper.

When talking to this same victim you may ask,

Police: "Did he ejaculate on you?"
Victim: "Huh??"
Police: "Did he skeet on you?"
Victim: "Yeah"

This is not the format that goes into writing on your report. Your report would read, "the victim stated the suspect ejaculated on her." Even though she used the word "skeet," that was the language necessary for the officer to use to talk on a level the victim could understand.

Street language will probably be new to you and you will need a translation for some cultures. Don't try to look some of the words or phrases up in the dictionary, they won't be there. Get a definition from your partner if you have to.

Once you are satisfied you have the specifics about the offense, remove the single, solitary, new notepad.

Begin writing on the front of the first page only. Do not flip the page and write on the back. Do not open the notepad in the center and begin to write. Write only from the front to the back of the notepad and on the top page. Remain organized; use one page for each complainant or witness's information.

You will need the complainant's full name and have them spell it. Are they a Jr. or a Sr., this can make a tremendous difference come arrest time. Their date of birth. Their current address usually with the zip code. The phone numbers they can be reached at and one they can be reached at during the day. If the person you are dealing with is transient, meaning they are staying with a girlfriend this week but next week....? Get this person's mother's address. If they move around a lot and are in and out of jail you can contact their mother. Mother's always know where their babies are!

This is important for the latent investigator who usually works the day shift. Your detectives will be completing a follow up if necessary and will need daytime numbers for efficiency. Work information including address, phone numbers and times and days they are working, also get the occupation of the person you are speaking with. Some reports require social security numbers and some others require driver's license numbers. Obtain whichever your department requires.

This is the basic information you will need on each person you are speaking with regardless of his or her role in the offense. Whether they are the victim, witness, suspect, or defendant, make this procedure of obtaining information an immediate habit. Stay organized and remain consistent as to how you write this information on your notepad. Label each person's role, such as victim, complainant, witness, suspect or defendant next to his or her name. Write a brief interview as to what they saw, heard or watched. After a few interviews this will become a procedure that you are very comfortable with and will be able to complete very quickly.

Use additional pages in the notepad for more details on interviews, just remember to label the pages, put the person's name and also their role in the offense.

Sample Notepad

Victim:

W/F Cootchie, Hutch E.
1710 N. Tampa Street
Tampa, FL 33602
Hm. Phone: 555-0217
Wk. Phone: 555-0198
411 Franklin Street

Occupation: Dancer

– Used drugs in club
– Argument w/another w/f dancer "Shashay"
– Hit from behind and choked with a g-string. Didn't see who!

Draw diagrams on the notepad of crime scenes and traffic crash accident scenes. You can also draw pictures of missing jewelry and any other unique items that may not have a serial number.

Basic information you need to obtain is very consistent and you will begin to sound like you are asking the same questions over and over. That's fine. Investigations, except for a few minor adjustments, are almost identical. People are spoken to, asked questions of, walked around with. Some will give you information in an articulate manner and some will be very unorganized. Both types will have to be assisted to make sure they are giving you complete information. Some will be easier than others.

Unfortunately a person's level of intelligence does not have a thing to do with their ability to recall details for you. You will have to pry information out of some. Others simply will not stop talking. Depending on the geographics of your area, witnesses come in all shapes and sizes.

Need suspect clothing descriptions? Teenage girls are great at this. Need suspect vehicle information? Teenage boys know them all and can probably give you the rim and tire type too. High crime neighborhood? Hundreds of people standing around, but no one saw a thing? Come back later and ask the old woman on the porch. She sees everything but will not volunteer if you don't ask.

New to a high prostitution area? Get to know the prostitutes and transvestites in the area. Tell them you are new and want to practice a field information report on them. Tell them you may need to know who to call for them if they get hurt or worse. They understand this, many are found dead with no I.D. and it takes days to identify and notify the family. Well-known and accepted job hazard. When talking to people of this profession they may give you a street name. Especially the men. If you encounter a 6', 4" black "female" with an Adams apple, razor stubble, 3" long red fingernails and a waist length black curly wig, and they tell you their name is Diana, call them Diana. Chat with them, let them know you know they are "working" but you are not here to arrest them. Then don't. Nod to them occasionally as you drive by. If you ever need to know the word on the street you now have someone you can approach that you know, sort of. This can go a long way in solving crimes or just finding out what is going on in certain neighborhoods.

This will not work with street level drug dealers however; they are historically anti-police and have no desire to assist you in your investigation. The only time I was able to enlist the aid of dealers was when a small child was missing. I pulled right up to a group of them. Several rode off on bikes, some ran. The ones that were not holding drugs stayed. As I described my extremely urgent problem to them, these dealers called the others back. They described the child and sent the dealers out to assist with the search. The child was found 10 minutes later, by a dealer on a bike who brought her back to me on his handlebars. I was touched by his concern for the little girl, until he asked me if there was a reward he could collect!

Always remember, when talking to people and gathering information, to notice your crime scene. With time you will learn what to look for at most scenes. Advanced training classes will teach you what to look for at homicide scenes, traffic crashes, injury investigations, child abuse and many other types of offenses.

Begin, prior to these advanced classes, to form a habit of asking the complainant, during the walk through, what certain things are. Such as, was this window already broken? Was this furniture already tipped over? Did the car come to rest that way or did someone move it? What are those injuries from, a hand or an object? What type of object? Where is it now? Is the injury a cut, an abrasion, a bruise, or a puncture wound? When looking at a bullet hole, find out if you are looking at an entry wound or an exit wound. If the victim is still alive and conscious this is easy, ask them. However, if the victim is dead, don't go into detail about what the mark is, or what it is from. (more on this in the legal chapter)

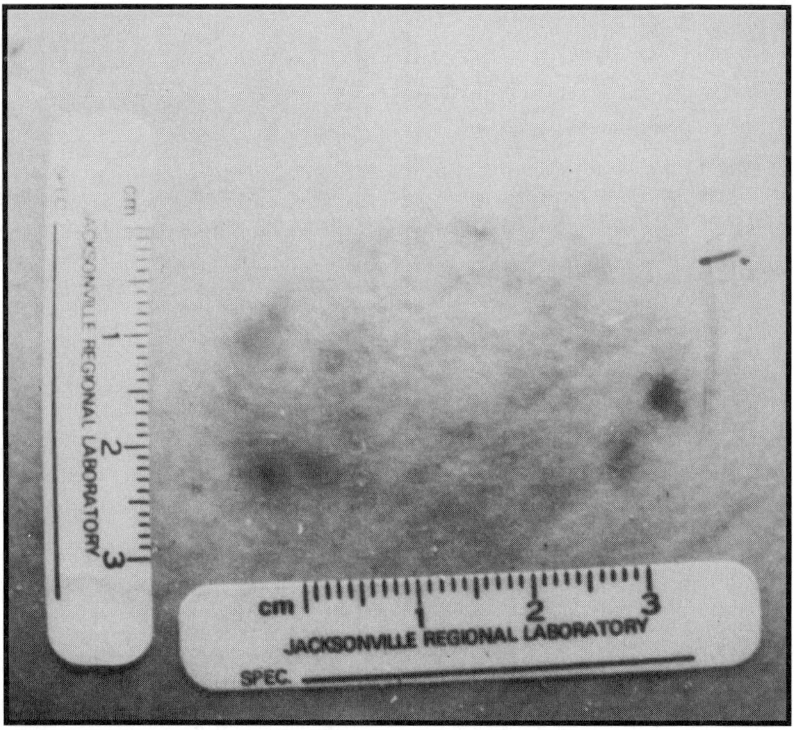

Again, it is ok to ask your complainant, victim or witness, these types of questions. Physical evidence does not lie, but you could spend all day trying to analyze skid marks to come up with a possible scenario when the witness that "saw the whole thing" is standing there waiting to talk to someone. Beware of the jr. detective that thinks they saw the whole thing and just wants to talk. This will become apparent as you try to match up their story with the physical evidence, something will not fit, find a new witness.

There are always two sides to every story. Human nature dictates that we will believe the first story we hear. If that first story is backed by a second person telling the similar story, it becomes the truth. Be careful. Find the second person that was actually involved. Check your physical evidence to make sure everything matches up.

I proved this to myself in a domestic violence situation. I was called, by the neighbors of a victim, to come to the neighbor's home. When I got there the victim was laying on the floor, bleeding from her mouth. She had obviously been hit in the mouth and had cuts on her lips.

The victim told me she came home late and her husband went into a rage and punched her in the mouth with his fist. She was little, 5' nothing and, 90 pounds fully dressed. Her husband, according to her, was 6'4" and 250 with a muscular build and was an angry white male.

Now, I am a highly trained police officer. I was a defensive tactics instructor, but I still got thrown around a lot. I know my limitations. I asked for not one, but two more back up units to respond. The victim had given me probable cause to arrest the husband for hitting her and I was going to go get the bad guy and really teach him a lesson about hitting little women.

I waited outside; my back up was slow in responding. While I was waiting, the bad guy came outside and looked around. I tried to watch him without him seeing me. I tried to melt into the tree bark I was standing next to. No luck. He saw me and casually walked up to me. He said, "I guess you're here for me, aren't you?" He was contrite, demure and very unaggressive. Not at all like the victim described him. Since my back up was not there yet I decided to take advantage of his talkative nature. I told him I was conducting the investigation and I wanted to get his side of the story, looking over my shoulder for the back up, nowhere in sight. Talking to him was one of my better moves and taught me a very valuable lesson.

His story was as follows: The victim was threatening to leave him for months. She was out tonight with "someone" and got drunk. She came home drooling and staggering, and he yelled at her for driving drunk. A small matter she forgot to mention to me. He said she told him to get out, he said no. He told the victim to calm down or he would call her adult son to come and get her. He had the cordless phone in his hand, ready to call. She grabbed the phone from him and they had a pulling match over the phone. He didn't want to fight with her and released the phone. She pulled one last time and popped herself in the mouth with the phone. Then she threw the phone at him. He ducked and turned away, she jumped on him as he turned away and scratched his back. He showed me the red welts from her fingernails. Well, this is a slightly different version. And my physical evidence is leaning toward his story. But I wanted more. I asked if there were any witnesses. Yep, his two kids, ages 8 and 9 watched the entire exchange. Even though I was leaning toward his story now, I wanted to confirm everything. I spoke with his two kids. They were separated and neither could hear the other. They did not hear their dad's story, as we spoke outside. They both showed me the dent in the drywall where she threw the phone. They both mentioned her smacking herself in the mouth with the phone and her scratching their dad, on his back. Both told me they knew she was going to try to leave their dad, even though dad had tried to keep it quiet. Both kids were very mature and had seen a little too much in their short lives, right in their own living room, all at the hands of their stepmother. By the way, my back up was not there yet.

I went back to the neighbors home, to the victim. She was being patched up by fire rescue. I asked her if she was going to go to the hospital or if she wanted to stay home. She said now that I had arrested her husband, she would stay home. I helped the paramedics gently lift her to her feet, turned her around and quickly snapped a set of handcuffs on her and took her to jail.

She had given me probable cause to place her husband under arrest for spouse battery. She had injuries and she made me believe her story, because it was first. If my back up had been there early I would have simply handcuffed the bad guy quickly, to avoid a fight and would not have had the opportunity to walk around his home for the tour of the crime scene. I would have been very, very wrong!!!

There is always another side to every story, find that other side and try to remain impartial. Human nature makes that hard to do, remember that. And also remember, everyone likes to lie to the police!! Well, most do anyway.

Physical evidence is anything you can see, but sometimes it will be invisible to the naked eye, items such as skid marks, hair fibers, and blood. Some will become permanent and some will go away after it rains or is disturbed. Document the physical evidence, its location and what it is, or from. Make arrangements to have the evidence photographed prior to moving it. The evidenciary value is lost if someone at your scene picks the gun up examines it and puts it down in the exact same spot. Staff members are always good for this and a good kick of shell casings too.

If your scene is a serious one, meaning someone died or may die, or whatever your department dictates as serious, close the scene off. Use that giant roll of yellow crime scene tape, just like you see on T.V. and wrap it up. This will usually be the rookie's job, so be ready.

Determine the size of the scene. Point various objects out to the originating officer, from there to there? If in doubt make it bigger, you can always shrink it later. The tape is not permanent. You usually cannot enlarge the scene especially after the encroaching crowd stomps on your blood trail. Use utility poles, car antennas, side view mirrors and the like. Tie it off and pull it tight. The tape stretches and is hard to break by pulling. Make it about waist, to mid chest high.

I have no idea why the tape is so effective but if you tell a group of bystanders, "don't step off the curb" and you have no other barrier the crowd will eventually end up in the middle of the street. Crime scene tape is just a thin, plastic strip. The crowd will come up to, touch but will not cross the tape. Usually they will not even push on it. Psychologically tape is a powerful tool for crowd control. **Caution: it becomes thin, plastic tape again in the event of civil unrest.

Your next job as the "rookie" officer will be the control log or the crime scene list. As mentioned previously the "Brass" is always good for kicking shell casings. They are also excellent crime scene destruction teams. They will enter your scene regardless of the severity and stomp, scuff and spit, drop gum wrappers and generally be useless and in the way waiting for the news cameras to show up. Then they will huddle, and look serious pretending to know what is going on and discussing the best course of action to take. To prevent this from happening, get your clipboard. Attach a piece of paper and begin writing down names. From the mayor and his wife all the way down to the crime scene technician. Everyone gets his or her name added to the report as being inside the crime scene. This is correct, accurate and the best method of weeding out the useless from your scene. If you are at the scene prior to the evidence destruction teams' arrival, all the better. If that clipboard is there first, they will not come in!

A sample Crime Scene Log follows.

Generic Police Report

Crime Scene Log	7 NOV 00	
Name:	IN	OUT
Ofc. Frendleigh	1940 hrs	2120 hrs
Ofc. Schmuchayer	1940 hrs	2120 hrs
Rescue # 4 Blud	1945 hrs	1955 hrs
Rescue # 4 Guttes	1945 hrs	1955 hrs

Crime Scene Log	7 NOV 00	
Sgt. So. Smart	1950 hrs	2120 hrs
Chief E. Weify	2000 hrs	2002 hrs
Medical Examiner, Gory	2030 hrs	2100 hrs
Crime Lab Tech, Dusty	2035 hrs	2100 hrs

A special note in dealing with the press. Members of the press listen to police and fire scanners, and show up to your most important scenes almost as fast as you do. They do not have access to your crime scene. They will try to lift the tape and come in, saying "press" and try to breeze by you looking as if they know what they are doing. Remove them. Direct them to a predetermined location and let them know the PIO (Public Information Officer) or Chief or other important person will be with them shortly. They do not have a right to enter an active scene and they will try to intimidate you into feeling you are doing something wrong by denying them admittance. Do not budge. Do not give interviews and do not say anything off-color or anything that could be taken out of context. Those giant antennas on the roofs of the vans that go up 40-50 feet are sensitive microphones. Also be aware some will point their cameras at you, turn them on and walk away. Treat every camera as if it is on and recording. Otherwise you will see yourself on the evening news laughing about the gross condition of the dead body and looking very insensitive and foolish.

Police officers use humor as a way to relieve stress. Crime scenes involving death can cause stress in some officers and we may not realize it. We make sick comments about positions of bodies and laugh at the grotesque details. This is very common for emergency personnel, but very difficult to explain to the public.

When all the excitement dies down and the scene is secure, have your FTO show you around. When a piece of evidence is found, ask questions, why, what makes that look like that? Have everything explained to you, this is your training phase, your sole purpose is to learn. Ask, or the FTO may assume you already know and you could miss valuable information. If your FTO is familiar with your Detectives and Medical Examiners, ask to follow them around. Tell them who you are and ask them questions. Some of the better ones will appreciate this and be flattered by your interest and will give you vast amounts of information. Some are simply jerks and will not speak to you.

After you have completed your interviews, surveyed the crime scene, dusted for fingerprints, photographed and collected evidence, completed rough drawings, observed injuries, measured skid marks and feel you have enough information to put together the entire scenario in your head, with no gaps left, no major questions left unanswered, you are ready to write your police report.

Chapter Three
"Full Report on my Desk in the Morning!"

Now is the time we can slow down and sit down. Pour yourself a tall cup of java and treat yourself to a big "all the way bagel" (cops don't eat doughnuts anymore). Find a safe place to write, probably in your police car and let's begin.

The police report is going to be the "story" told by you, the officer, about what happened. Some reports are going to be very lengthy and require extreme detail. Some others will be a simple fill in the blank with a short accompanying narrative.

When writing a police report there are only three basic areas that need to be completed.

- **First is the fill in the blank portion.**
- **Next will be the synopsis of the incident.**
- **On a lined page you will write, in narrative style, the investigation and any interviews you conducted.**

Most agencies have additional forms that go with certain types of offenses. Areas within and outside your department request these forms. Latent investigators and prosecutors use specialized forms to streamline and simplify the details needed by them for quicker action in follow up and filing charges.

When you write a police report and complete accompanying forms, there are a few basic guidelines that should be followed to help the handwritten reports look professional.

Make sure the pens you are carrying are black ink only. Use a block letter style when writing. Don't write in cursive, this looks amateurish and is sometimes difficult to read and decipher.

It is usually most efficient to begin writing on your department's primary police report, the face sheet, incident report or offense report. The reason for this is all of your collected information will go on this report in an organized format. You can put the information down in a fill in the blank style in a few minutes. Referring back to find any necessary information will be easy by looking it up on the report rather than sifting through your notepad.

First you will want to briefly go over your notes on your notepad. Assemble the paperwork and accompanying forms that will be needed to complete the report for your offense.

LOCATION

To begin with, the fill in the blank portion of the main police report determines the exact location the offense occurred. When writing out the locations remember to be very specific in writing direction and street or avenue.

2739 N. 25th Street

vs.

2739 E. 25th Avenue

In the city I work in the direction, meaning north, south, east and west. Street or avenue need to be specifically documented. If the locations are not separated then we are writing about two different locations, several blocks from one another but no one will know which one. Try explaining that one in court 3 years later.

Don't forget to get the apartment numbers. Some people assume you know when they do or do not live in an apartment and they also think the apartment number is not important. Always ask for one, just in case.

DATES

When writing out the date there are several accepted methods. Your department may have their own requirements, basically 05May00, or 05-05-00, are acceptable and fit in the tiny allotted space provided by most reports.

TIME

When documenting time most agencies require the use of military time to alleviate the confusion of night and day offenses. Military time begins at one minute after midnight with the time written as 0001 hrs. One a.m. is shown as 0100 hrs. Noon is shown as 1200 hrs and one in the afternoon is shown as 1300 hrs. Keep counting around the clock until you come back to midnight with the time of 2400 hrs. Military time will be standard for most police reports except those reports that are regularly handed out to civilians. Those reports will be traffic crash reports and traffic tickets, summons to appear for arraignments and the like. On these reports there is usually a prompt to remind you to use "regular people time." This prompt is the simple _______a.m. or _______p.m.

COMPLAINANT

Next determine who your complainant is. This will be the person or entity that has the most damage or loss, the victim listed does not necessarily have to be a person. This may seem cruel but in the event of an armed robbery, the clerk that had a shotgun shoved into their face, but was not injured, is not the primary victim. The convenience store, losing money in the robbery, will be listed as the primary victim. The convenience store clerk that was on the scene, that you actually spoke to, will be listed as the second victim.

Some offenses will have multiple victims with injuries. The victim with the most severe injury will be the first victim listed.

PROPERTY

When documenting, under the stolen items section, property that has been taken, there are a few things to be aware of.

You will not have had any training on how to determine the value of items taken. People really believe that the dollar amount that is put onto a police report is the amount their insurance company will pay them for their "stuff" that was stolen. Sometimes they may tend to embellish a little when describing the items and telling you their value.

All a police officer is required to put on a police report to document the value of an item that was stolen is, fair market value. That's not third world country, trade embargo, triple digit inflation fair market value. We are looking for simple, ordinary U.S. fair market value.

Emotional value is of no consequence when reporting theft to police. The 87 year old crime victim that told you her two pet parakeets were stolen off her front porch and determines them to be priceless... Help her out. The pet store down the street sells them for $6.00 each. Put twelve dollars on your police report. The fact they were highly trained and able to squawk out the theme song from "Cops" does not add to their value.

In the same token the complainant that tells you his classic 1976 Zenith console television, with the built in 2 watt speakers and the original dial changer, cracked and yellowed slightly, is a collector's item, might require a professional opinion for fair market value.

If your offense if teetering on misdemeanor theft vs. felony theft and you just cannot fathom how the TV can be worth $2000.00, call your local used TV shop/repair guy and tell him who you are and what you have. Tell him you need a fair market value for the TV, and use his numbers.

Each agency will have their own style of fill in the blank format. Your FTO can assist you in the exact requirements for your agency. Since we followed the basic procedures in the previous chapter, all the necessary information to complete the blanks will be in your hand in your single notebook.

PAGE NUMBERS

An additional note, do not put page numbers on any of the report pages yet. We could have a lot to write, multiple pages is a common occurrence and we will wait to put page numbers on as the last task.

SYNOPSIS

When you have completed the fill in the blank portion of your report you will have come across a section for the synopsis of the report. The purpose of the synopsis, usually located on the front page, is to alert the reader of the basic content of the report. This is the area that will be read first, to determine if the report is going to be interesting enough to continue, or sign and send on.

The synopsis is usually formatted as a brief statement of the facts of the incident. Only five or six lines are provided for this area, it is meant to be brief. If you write on all the lines, you are working way too hard. When completing this section do not repeat any information already provided in the fill in the blank section. You will want to describe your incident in the briefest manner possible. Finally, justify the title of the report by describing how the offense met the charging statutes or codes. Confused?

Don't be, this is simple and I am going to give you a basic standard format that can have a word or two changed. This will allow you to adopt this format for almost all the synopsis' you will be writing.

As I mentioned before, probably the most common offense reported will be a burglary. Most states require a secondary offense, attempted, or intended, for the crime of burglary to be complete. To write a basic synopsis for the crime of burglary and include the criminal elements of the state statute or code, write a brief statement such as:

Generic Police Report

Synopsis:
Unknown suspect(s) forcibly entered the above
residence, took the listed property and fled,
undetected in an unknown direction.

This is the briefest possible way to say: Bad Guy(s) but we don't know who, broke into the complainants home took their stuff and got away.

And no one saw a thing.

This synopsis format can be changed easily to match your different crimes.

Car gets broken into? - Unknown suspect(s) forcibly entered the compl's car, took the listed property and fled undetected in an unknown direction.

Unknown can be changed to known, if the scenario fits, but don't put in the name of the bad guy, that will be in the section for arrests or suspects.

Forcibly can be changed to struck or hit if your crime is any type of an assault/battery, and so on.

Generally the synopsis will be very short. If additional details are required by your agency, put them in, this is just a basic formula to get you started easily and efficiently.

Burglary is an ideal investigation to work on as a new officer. The bad guy is usually gone by the time police arrive. The investigation is done at your own pace. The bad guy leaves all kinds of great physical evidence to look at and study. The victims are usually not injured and will allow you to conduct your investigation. They are going to be annoyed but generally cooperative and will give you full access to their home to look for "clues."

NARRATIVE

After you have completed the fill in the blank portion and the synopsis, you will be ready for the narrative. When you begin documenting the incident in narrative space, which is usually the most difficult portion to get started on, you will want to remember a few pointers.

Narrative style is intimidating. It's a big blank page staring at you, waiting for you to ramble inefficiently, lose track of your chronological order, use too much white out, and have to tear it up and start over. It's easy to forget a detail from either the investigation or the interview and end up with a report that is disjointed and hard to follow. Putting the incident into chronological order is logical and the easiest to read. Even though you will receive information in a very unorganized manner, it is allowable and expected that you put it back into order for the reader.

Your narrative page will be a series of empty lines. You will want to begin each section of the narrative portion with a heading to identify what the reader is looking at. This will be Investigation and Interview.

INVESTIGATION

The investigation section will be written out in a narrative style and goes into detail about your actions at the scene. The investigation will be written in the first person. Meaning, I arrived, I saw, I heard, I watched.

This is the area that will tell the "story" of how you saw the call and all of your investigative actions, from the point of dispatch to the completion of what happened to bad guys, victims or witnesses. It will detail everything you personally did at the scene with relationship to the call.

Reading many reports from different agencies and receiving feedback from my students on what is the best way to document incidents, beginning with the investigation, is the hands down favorite.

Reading the investigation first allows the reader to get a full mental picture of what happened at the scene. The reader can then go thru the interviews of complainants and witnesses and read specifics about, and fully understand each person's role.

In organizing your thoughts for writing out an investigation here is a simple formula with a few elements for you to follow.

Begin by documenting on a narrative page:

THE HEADING

- *Investigation*
- *Interview*

Generic Police Report

Investigation:

It can become very important to document how you received your call. Did you roll up on it? Did radio or computer dispatch it? This is an element that is seldom documented. This is one of the first things an attorney will ask you on the stand. "Officer, how did you receive this call?" Two years later in court, on the witness stand, you will not remember this detail. It probably will not make a difference, legally one way or another. However, attorneys get paid to make you look dumb and the best place to do this is on the witness stand in front of an audience. They will exhale at you, look at you and give you a moment of silence and glance at the jury, rolling their eyes because you cannot answer this usually unimportant question. This makes you look incompetent on the first question, assuming you stated your name and occupation correctly. This is an ego killer for you and puts the defense attorney on a roll as being in the power position, to the jury.

Stop this one before it happens. Begin your narrative on your police report with a simple one liner:

HOW YOU RECEIVED THIS CALL

- *I received this call via voice dispatch. Or*
- *I received this call from computer dispatch. Or*
- *I observed this call in progress.*

However you got this call or information for this call, make that the first sentence of your Investigation. This automatically starts you in chronological order and creates a mental picture of where you were and what you were doing. It's also a simple, basic way to get things moving.

Generic Police Report

Investigation:
I received this call via voice dispatch.

The next element we will document is:

WHO YOU MET WITH, SPOKE WITH OR INTERVIEWED

This area is the most common area for mix ups. All we need to know is who spoke to who.

Using the simple one sentence format:

- *On my arrival I met with and interviewed the compl...* STOP.
- Many officers naturally want to continue with...*and she stated...*

What she stated would be listed in her interview. We will go into detail about how to complete her interview later.

If there were multiple interviews with additional officers assisting you, put that in the report...

- *I interviewed the compl. and Ofc. Frendleigh interviewed the witness.*

Generic Police Report

Investigation:
I received this call via voice dispatch. **On my arrival I**
met with and interviewed the compl.

The next element in your investigation will be the

IMMEDIATE ACTIONS TAKEN BY YOU

This element may not apply for all reports.

In the event of your arrival onto an injury scene you may be required to call for an ambulance.

If you arrive on this burglary and you see the bad guy running down the street carrying a VCR, you might have the uncontrollable urge to chase him. If the half price pasta dinner you just ate is still sticking to your ribs and you can't chase him, you will probably want to place an alert with your dispatcher for him on the radio.

Document your immediate actions or your response to emergency conditions, if there are any.

- *As I approached the complainant's home, I observed a bad guy run out the front door. He was carrying a VCR under his arm in a football type hold and fled south across the compl's yard toward the back of the house into an alleyway. I placed an alert on the radio for the suspect.*

Notice we did not document the suspect's description here. The description will go in the fill in the blank area...w/m 5' 9" medium build, you get the idea.

Or...

- *As I approached the compl's home I observed a severe paper cut on the compl's finger. I requested an ambulance to respond to the scene. Fire rescue unit #4 and engine #4 responded and placed the compl's finger into a splint.*

Again this specific element may not apply to all calls. Remember chronological order. Following chronological order simply allows you to recall, document and create a better mental picture in writing.

NEXT YOU WILL DESCRIBE WHAT YOU SAW WHEN YOU ARRIVED

This can be documented extensively for a homicide scene, or simply for a delayed offense that does not have much of a crime scene. Again the purpose here is to create a mental picture, in writing, to describe what the crime scene looked like.

Previously we discussed walking the complainant through the crime scene. For our sample burglary we will do the same. The compl knows her home better than anyone. Having her walk us through the home, showing us what is out of place, missing or in disarray is preferred.

Generic Police Report

Investigation:
I received this call via voice dispatch. On my arrival I
met with and interviewed the compl. **The compl.'s**
home was a one-story block structure. This home
faced west, toward the street. A solid core, wood
door faced the street and was located under a deep

overhanging roof that was enclosed by a screened
porch. Both the east and west sides of the porch
had very heavy planting materials, obscuring the
view from the sides. During the exterior search of
the home I observed a window on the west side of
the home. The sill of the window had two
handprints smeared in the dust, leaving a clean
spot with two visible fingerprints. This window
looked directly into the home and faced the TV
and VCR.

One tip to remember, when conducting this portion of the interview that will lead up to documentation under the investigation section is, you are the cop. The complainant is just a complainant.

If the complainant tells you she saw the bad guy run with the VCR, she watched the bad guy kick in the door, this will go into her interview. Remember, she saw, she watched, she heard...

If she tells you, "look, this is where they got in, they kicked the door in here," because she thinks so, because she saw the same type of a crime on TV last night...but she didn't witness it actually happen, tough. You're the cop!!

That's her job to point out what is out of place, but we determine what we are looking at and what "possibly" happened. We are the highly trained investigators and we will decide what really happened here, thank you very much!

In the legal chapter, I will explain why we don't assume and put that assumption in writing, why we don't want to give the bad guy an alibi, in writing, on an official police report, based on a possibly incorrect assumption.

INVESTIGATIVE ACTIONS

After the walk through with the complainant is finished, you will begin your investigative actions. This will include dusting for fingerprints, collecting evidence and so on; this will be documented next.

Generic Police Report

Investigation:
I received this call via voice dispatch. On my arrival I
met with and interviewed the compl. The compl.'s
home was a one-story block structure. This home
faced west, toward the street. A solid core, wood door
faced the street and was located under a deep
overhanging roof that was enclosed by a screened
porch. Both the east and west sides of the porch had
very heavy planting materials, obscuring the view from
the sides. During the exterior search of the home I

observed a window on the west side of the home.
The sill of the window had two handprints smeared
in the dust, leaving a clean spot with two visible
fingerprints. This window looked directly into the
home and faced the TV and VCR. **I processed the**
crime scene for fingerprints. Several were removed
from the interior, on top of the TV set, near the
VCR's previous location. Several fingerprints were
found on the freezer door. All prints were lifted and
sent to the lab for processing. The footprint on the
exterior door was photographed, both with a
measure and without.

Your academy training will have a class that covers what to look for in a crime scene. Through experience you will notice details that immediately tell you what may have happened. In many years of investigating offenses I noticed one thing. A pattern. Bad guys must have some sort of a training program all their own. Many burglary offenses are committed similarly and the same items taken over and over. Or maybe they are taking the easy way out.

Real bad guys don't usually wear gloves. They don't have fancy glass cutters or carry tool kits to bypass alarms and cut wires. Bad guys don't carry rappelling gear to make a fast getaway from the fifth floor mansion, in case they are detected by Bob the security guard in his fully equipped pursuit golf cart, and they don't crack safes. All this is true for the TV burglars. They are high class, cool, have neat stuff they carry with them and they always wear black turtleneck sweaters. They only hit the very rich in extremely daring, complicated heists and drive sports cars to the golf course during the day.

Real life, everyday burglars are sweaty, stinky, drug addicts that go from house to house looking for an unlocked door. They carry no fancy equipment and would probably hang themselves the first time they tried to escape by rappelling. They are opportunists. Prowling and looking in windows of a home, during the day when the homeowner is at work is a favorite. If they have the energy to kick in a door they will. But climbing in a window, if low enough, then walking out the door they can unlock from the inside, is usually the easiest.

Carrying the small items, VCR, jewelry and food from the freezer is accomplished by taking a pillowcase off the bed. Then like a skinny Santa Clause in July they pedal down the street on their stolen bike to the nearest crooked pawn shop.

These guys leave lots of evidence, some useful, some not. The print of the shoe can be photographed, for further use in case similar crimes occur. Interior surfaces, likely to have been touched when the stolen items were picked up, can be dusted for prints, too. Follow your department's policies and procedures in processing your crime scenes.

PERIMETER SEARCH

The last element we can mention is looking for the bad guy. In addition to the perimeter search we did around the compl's home, we can search further for the suspect.

Generic Police Report

Investigation:
I received this call via voice dispatch. On my arrival I
met with and interviewed the compl. The compl.'s
home was a one-story block structure. This home
faced west, toward the street. A solid core, wood door
faced the street and was located under a deep
overhanging roof that was enclosed by a screened
porch. Both the east and west sides of the porch had
very heavy planting materials, obscuring the view from
the sides. During the exterior search of the home I
observed a window on the west side of the home. The
sill of the window had two handprints smeared in the
dust, leaving a clean spot with two visible fingerprints.
This window looked directly into the home and faced
the TV and VCR. I processed the crime scene for
fingerprints. Several were removed from the interior, on
top of the TV set, near the VCR's previous location.
Several fingerprints were found on the freezer door. All
prints were lifted and sent to the lab for processing.
The footprint on the exterior door was photographed,

both with a measure and without. **The immediate area around the home was checked for signs of the suspect, with negative results. Nearby pawn shops were also checked, with negative results.**

This type of offense requires a quick hand off of merchandise. Bad guys don't take the VCR because they want to watch a good movie. They need their quick fix of narcotics. Selling the VCR in a crooked pawn shop for a quick twenty dollars is common. Also trading the VCR directly to the drug dealer is common.

A female police officer friend of mine working undercover as a drug dealer accepted a pair of high heeled shoes in exchange for a piece of crack cocaine. The officer studied the shoes, carefully turned them over and even tried them on and pranced and danced around and did a bump and grind to the heavy bass beat of a passing car's stereo. Then she gave the left/right "scan for police look," and handed the bad girl a piece of rock cocaine. Needless to say, we in the surveillance van were laughing so hard we almost missed the signal to call in the knock down unit.

If you have a good rapport with the pawn shops in the area, let them know what you are looking for. They don't want to accept stolen merchandise; they lose money, and might even call you if the bad guy walks in with the item you're looking for.

INTERVIEW

Previously we discussed talking to your complainant at the scene. We calmed them down, walked them to a safe area, called them an ambulance for their paper cut and finally had them walk us through the crime scene. We distinguished the difference between what they saw and what they wanted to see.

From this walk through we have determined the basic information that was needed for the fill in the blank part of our report. The complainant gave us the required information to write a synopsis and combining the walk thru and the interview, we completed the investigation.

Now we are ready to write the interview.

Generic Police Report

Interview:

If your complainant watched an offense occur you could potentially have a very lengthy interview telling a nice detailed "story" of what happened. It will be written through their eyes, but in your words. However, in this type of delayed, did not witness, burglary, the interview will be quite small.

The interview is the area in which each complainant, witness, defendant or whomever else, will get to have their story put down in writing. The interview will detail everything the complainant said, saw, watched, heard, did or knew.

Most agencies will have an accepted format that allows each individual involved to have their own interview listed separately from the others.

You will write this in the third person. Meaning, they said, they saw, they heard, they did, what they knew.

This is an area that will need some pruning. Not everything the complainant says will be important.

To assist you in determining what is of importance, you can follow a simple formula.

This formula was developed so the interview covers areas that it needs to include for the complainant to be a legal witness, and to include elements for charging a bad guy with a crime. The formula also helps you to feel comfortable in throwing out the garbage and rambling the complainant probably did during your interview.

- **Each interview will be separate from the other, and each will have their own heading with the name and role of the person's involvement in the crime.**

Generic Police Report

Interview: **Compl. (A. R. Head)**

In the interview we will need to know certain elements, just like we did for the investigation.

Complainants will give you the information you need to help conduct your investigation. But some of the information you receive will be of no use what so ever. Through experience you will be able to immediately determine what the verbal junk is and mentally discard it from your memory. You will hear all about how a person is on medication and this crime has traumatized them. They have their own versions of how a crime was committed and why. They just saw on TV a bad guy did some outlandish crime and they think it has just happened to them too. Lots of information will need to be pushed aside.

The elements that we need to know to write an interview start with the element that was mentioned in the second chapter.

WHERE WAS THE COMPLAINANT WHEN THIS OFFENSE STARTED?

Again this begins chronological order for the complainant and for your report. It creates a mental picture for the reader as to the complainant's location and begins the paragraph smoothly.

Generic Police Report

Interview: Compl. (A. R. Head)
The victim said she left her home to go to work at
approx. 0700 hrs this morning.

During the investigation you will ask the complainant basic questions such as, were the doors locked? Did anyone have access to the home? Does/did she have a roommate?

Each investigation will have its own bank of questions. The questions, regardless of the offense being reported, work toward the common and ultimate goal of proving the elements for the statute were met. The next goal is, what's the easiest way to find the bad guy?

When writing the report you will not write out the questions you asked the complainant. You will want to document their answers only, in a narrative format. This is an area of "assumability." The readers of the police report will read the interview and will be able to know what question was asked, by the answer given. You are basically documenting the answers in statement format.

The next element that needs to be documented is

WHAT THE COMPLAINANT KNEW

Generic Police Report

Interview: Compl. (A. R. Head)
The victim said she left her home to go to work at
approx. 0700 hrs this morning. **The compl. locked all**
doors and windows prior to leaving today.

Generic Police Report

Interview: Compl. (A. R. Head)
The victim said she left her home to go to work at
approx. 0700 hrs this morning. The compl. locked all
doors and windows prior to leaving today. **The compl.**
does not have a roommate and no one else has
access to the home.

Next document

WHAT THE VICTIM SAW OR WATCHED

For our burglary the complainant saw nothing. This part of the narrative would be left out and not acknowledged.

However, if the complainant came home and saw the bad guy run from the home with the VCR under his arm, that observation would be documented.

Example:

- *The compl. drove her car into her parking space on the east side of her home. As she was driving in she noticed a bad guy run out of her front door carrying what appeared to be a piece of electronic equipment. The bad guy ran south past the neighbors yard and into the alleyway.*

This area will be the most detailed if you are writing out the interview for a witness or a complainant that saw the offense occur.

When documenting this part of the interview be careful on the overuse of pronouns. Any interview that describes what happened with an offense involving many players can become very confusing.

Example:

- *The compl. watched him go up to him and beat him with the baseball bat. Then he ran from him toward him. He was stopped by the rest of them and they hit him again.*

Also avoid the use of the participant's names. We don't know the people involved and it becomes a page flipping disaster as the reader has to continually go back to the front page or next page to reread the name of the person involved just to understand their role in the offense you are reporting.

Example:

- *White watched Brown go up to Green and beat Green with a baseball bat. Then Brown ran up to White. Green was grabbed by the remaining Greens and was beaten black and blue.*

Naming all the people involved also defeats the purpose of keeping the identity of witnesses and victims involved confidential. If the report is handed out, it is very easy for a name in the body of the report to become public accidentally. This is a violation of criminal law in most states. We will go into privacy issues in depth in the legal chapter.

When writing out a lengthy report use the title of the person's **role** in the offense, not their name. If your interview has many people involved it will become a mix of he, she, they or "who's that bad guy" with too many names to remember. Stop the complainant on each pronoun and ask them to specify who; the name and role are needed.

Example:

- *The witness watched the defendant go up to the victim and beat the victim with a baseball bat. Then the defendant ran toward the witness. The victim was grabbed by the remaining defendant's and the victim was beaten again.*

If your incident has more than one victim you can identify them by calling them victim #1 and victim #2.

CLOSURE

A very important element you will always want to document, if the complainant did witness the offense is; can the complainant, or witness or victim, identify the bad guy?

IDENTIFICATION

We are not asking them to give us a name or the bad guys address. All we need to know is can the complainant recognize the bad guy if they see him again?

Generic Police Report

Interview: Compl. (A. R. Head)
The victim said she left her home to go to work at
approx. 0700 hrs this morning. The compl. locked all
doors and windows prior to leaving today. The compl.
does not have a roommate and no one else has
access to the home. a roommate and no one else has
access to the home. **The compl. cannot identify the**
suspect, but does wish to prosecute if a suspect is
found.

PROSECUTION

Most states require the complainant to specify if they want to prosecute or not. Only a few offenses are automatically prosecuted by states and automatically make the victim the witness for the state, without regard for their wishes. These offenses are domestic violence type offenses and of course murder.

For most other offenses you will need to specify the wishes of the complainant on the report. This will be a time saver in the referral and filing of charges. Detectives and prosecutors are busy enough without contacting their potential complainant and finding out they never wanted to prosecute anyway, they just needed a police report for their insurance.

Add the sentence as the last line of the complainant's interview. Combining the above two elements finishes the report neatly and leaves no doubt as to the interview being complete.

Example:

- *The complainant can identify the suspect and **does** want to prosecute.*

Or

- *The complainant can identify the suspect but **does not** wish to prosecute at this time.*

This is where the statute of limitations for your reported offense comes into effect. If the complainant has a neighbor that broke into her shed and took the lawnmower, but has decided not to prosecute, that's fine. The statute of limitations on a burglary is, in some states, 3 years. Within those three years the complainant has the ability to contact the prosecutors office and have charges filed against the bad guy and a warrant issued. Usually the police will not be involved in these types of delayed cases. But it is our job to write a complete police report for the complainant, even if we know it is going nowhere, for the time being.

Chapter Four Grammar and Spelling

A refresher for the old guys

Fortunately, for most police officers and their agencies, perfect sentence structure, syntax and grammar are not primary issues in report writing. I have trained many recruit police officers that led you to believe, through their writing, they did not graduate from high school, let alone attend a school that taught English. Let's face it, most of us got into this job because we knew we would get paid to drive fast and shoot guns. Those who wanted to blow stuff up, went into the military.

Most of the people, already outlined in this book that will read your police reports were not English experts either. They went into law school and criminal justice careers and had the same classes in English the rest of us did. Some a long time ago, some not.

To appease the reader that may know a little about English and how it is supposed to be written correctly, this chapter is for your benefit. This book is not based on how to write the perfect paper and I wouldn't know a participle, past or present, if it bit me. However, I do know that a highly trained police officer or detective who has cunning investigative skills, intuitive interview techniques and the brawn to catch bad guys does not want to ruin their image by writing like a ten year old in a remedial phonics class. This chapter is also for you.

First we will review the very basic English skills that we might actually use. I will pepper them with some ridiculous examples, to make them memorable. We will finish up quickly and then rush to the next chapter before you fall asleep with your nose pinched in the binder of this book.

SPELLING

Probably the most common writing error police officers make is misspelled words. This is an easy fix. As I mentioned in the previous chapter, if your spelling is bad get an automatic speller. This handy little device makes you look like a champ in seconds and smooths out the most common complaint made toward police reports. It fits in your uniform pocket and is readily available anytime you write.

PARAGRAPHS

Another common error is police officers tend to write an entire investigation in one paragraph. Don't forget, a paragraph is the description of a single idea. Paragraphs can, and should be written so they relate to one another. Luckily we accomplish this by using chronological order. It's okay to write an interview or an investigation combining many paragraphs. In police reports this will mean write out a paragraph for one area then a paragraph for another area, thought or idea. I'll show you what I mean.

Example:

The suspect prowled stealthily into the yard of the home. The suspect broke the upper part of the window out using a rock from the nearby herb garden. The suspect then reached into the window and slid open the lock. Once the suspect opened the window all the way, he got onto his tiptoes and looked inside.

The suspect then put his foot against the exterior of the wall of the home, directly under the window. He put his hands on the windowsill and pulled himself inside the window, using his foot on the outside wall as leverage.

Once inside the home, the suspect walked the entire home scanning for the room's valuables. The suspect removed a pillowcase from the bed in the master bedroom and placed the VCR into the pillowcase. He also helped himself to the frozen steaks in the freezer, placing them in the pillowcase.

The suspect unlocked the front door, swung the pillowcase up onto his shoulder and walked out, squinting and grinning in the bright sunlight.

For the purposes of a police report that is handwritten, you may indent the first word of the paragraph or simply drop down a line and begin a new sentence. This makes the break in the reading of the sentence, creates a natural pause and allows the reader to easily absorb the next series of events.

SENTENCE PARTS

When you are creating the sentence that builds your paragraphs, there are lots of rules and regulations that you must remember to write complete sentences. Avoid inexact pronoun reference, and always strive for the best use of transitional words to achieve coherence. Okay, I don't know what this really means. I do know that the easiest way to write, so that the subjects and predicates all agree, is to write like you talk.

We all had the English classes where we would identify parts of a sentence by underlining the words. The verb, or action word was underlined twice. This was the word that said what you did, action you took and so on. Remember your teacher saying, "if you can do it, it's a verb"?

In this same class we were supposed to identify the noun or the subject of the sentence, and underline it one time. Remember "people, place or thing?"

To write a complete sentence that reads smoothly you will have a verb and a noun. A subject and a predicate. If you do not have these two very basic elements present the sentence will not be complete. This is easy to tell because you will read the sentence and look for the rest, the conclusion or the finish. Writing a sentence without a subject or a predicate feels, sounds and reads unnaturally.

Example:

The suspect bled heavily from the bullet hole in his leg.

Our sentence has the noun or the subject (the suspect) and the verb or the action (bled).

An area in writing that a police officer can have a lot of fun is the use of adjectives. Those are the describer words used to describe nouns and pronouns. They also enhance action words.

Use adjectives to describe crime scenes and make the details come alive to the reader.

Example:

The screaming, writhing, agonized suspect bled thick, dark, sticky, crimson blood from the shredded, ragged bullet hole in his emaciated, waxy colored leg.

I think you get the idea on adjectives.

PUNCTUATION

When you write a sentence that will have many adjectives to describe and create that clear, concise mental picture, you will need to use punctuation for the benefit of the reader.

As you see above, when describing the suspect's blood, thick, dark, sticky, crimson they were separated by commas. This was done so that each describer was known to be separate. If commas were not used, or used incorrectly the sentence may read, "thick, dark, sticky crimson." What is sticky crimson? I don't know and I'm sure I could not tell a jury what it is either.

Additional punctuation that will be used within a sentence is the apostrophe. Apostrophes are used to show possession, as in who's what?

Example:

The suspect's leg

Apostrophes are also used when a contraction is written. Contraction, not meaning time them, breathe, and push, but an apostrophe used in place of a letter to form a word called a contraction.

Contractions are formed when a pronoun and a verb are combining to form a new word.

Example:

It is	becomes	*it's*
She is	becomes	*she's*
He is	becomes	*he's*
Do not	becomes	*don't*

And so on. Basically, if a letter can be removed and an apostrophe added, and it's still a real word, you have just formed a contraction.

Another bit of punctuation that will be used in police report writing is the quotation mark. This is a form of punctuation that we will use frequently and will absolutely need to be used correctly for legal purposes.

Remember when we used the example in the previous chapter of the victim describing how the suspect "skeeted" on her? If the person you are talking to, regardless of their role in any offense, uses a direct quote, it should go into quotation marks on your report. Now, not everything the person says is important enough to require the use of quotations. Save them for repeated quotes that the bad guy said to the victim.

Example:

The suspect told us to, "freeze, and get in the freezer."

Use them for when a person is describing street terminology to you, and it is their language.

Example:

He "skeeted" on me.

These types of street terminology used will need to be smartened up by a qualifier such as (common street term for ejaculation) written into the report.

By the way (these) are called parentheses. Use them for stepping aside to explain something.

If the crime you are investigating is any type of hate crime or one that can be considered one by your state laws, it will be very important to put into quotations the exact statements made to the victim by the bad guy, and overheard by any witnesses.

HEARSAY

On a side note, hearsay is allowed to be written into a police report. Make sure the hearsay is clearly documented as "overheard by the victim." Hearsay is when the victim heard what the bad guy said and told you. If we repeat what the bad guy told the victim we might be objected to and the statements stricken in court, or even a mistrial. (A mistrial means everyone goes home, and the whole process starts again) However, the victim heard, directly, what the bad guy said, (to him or overheard him) so the victim may be able to repeat what the bad guy said, in open court.

You, the officer will probably not be allowed to testify to the hearsay. Since the victim that heard the statement could, for the victim's benefit, and the benefit of successful prosecution, assist the victim. Write the victim or witnesses interview and put the important hearsay statements in quotes. The victim will be able to refresh from your police report in court prior to testifying.

Consistency is always best when testifying, especially with an inexperienced witness that is easily intimidated by a defense attorney.

SLANG AND #@$* ALSO KNOWN AS _ _ _ _!

Also, make sure any offensive words used by a suspect, are put into quotations.

Example:

The suspect called the victim a "damn whore" as the suspect beat the victim's head with the tire iron.

What we are trying to avoid is having the reader believe we, the police officer, chose to write using slang, swear, or any other offensive language.

This area will need some common sense in writing. Not every offensive word will need to be documented. And as you will find out, some of the people you come into contact with use *&$#@ as their everyday adjectives to talk about almost any subject.

MORE PUNCTUATION

When ending the sentence and beginning to write the next thought, remember to end the sentence with the ordinary old period.

Another ending you can use is an exclamation point! This is the equivalent to shouting in writing, use it accordingly.

Using a question mark is not something you will be doing a lot? No, really? Yes? I mean, no?

RUN ON SENTENCE

Ending the sentence is as easy as finishing the thought, phrase or statement. This is the natural pause in the sentence that completes the idea. It is very difficult to write an incomplete sentence, but very easy to write a run-on sentence. When describing an action, series of events, or statement, a run on sentence is hard to avoid.

When you have completed your thought and want to put it down on paper but you're not sure if it will end up in a run on, break the thought in two.

Example:

The suspect told the victims and witnesses to "freeze and get into the freezer," and then the suspect opened the cash register drawer and took all of the cash including the bait money.

Break this thought in two at the natural pause that describes the suspect's second act. Do this by replacing the comma with the ordinary period and capitalizing the first word of the next sentence.

Example:

The suspect told the victims and witnesses to, "freeze and get in the freezer." The suspect then opened the cash register drawer and took all of the cash including the bait money.

When your report is complete, proofread your final result.

If you run out of breath before you get to the period, that's a sign of a run-on sentence.

MORE SENTENCE PARTS

Next, we will talk about the use of pronouns. Pronouns may be used in the place of a noun. They are such words as I, you, he, she, it, we, and they.

Remember when we talked about interviewing the witnesses and having them stop and describe each person's involvement in the offense? We will receive the information as, "he did then he did then he did." Was the story being told to us talking about three men, or one? Have the witness clarify how many.

When writing the report remember to not repeat the same error to the reader that the witness did to us. We were there, we had the victim clarify who all the various "he's" were. It's easy to forget and write a police report with "he did then he did then he did." However, the readers question will be the same, "one subject or three?"

Avoid the overuse of pronouns. Instead use the person's **role** in the offense. "The **suspect** did then the **victim** did then the **witness** did."

CAPITALS

If you are unsure which words need to be capitalized and which don't, there are lots of rules for this subject too. Titles need to be capitalized, names, beginnings of sentences, street names, people's names and positions, and offenses. The easiest way to get around this is, as mentioned previously, write in all caps. Problem solved.

MORE THAN ONE, MAYBE?

Sometimes you will write about a person regarding details that are unknown. When you are writing about the unknown suspect that committed a crime, but we don't know how many suspects, or if there was more than one, do this. Write suspect(s). This shows maybe one maybe more. We are not limiting ourselves, legally, in writing to the possibility of just one bad guy.

This (s) is left for the unknown. Writing victim(s) when we know we have two is incorrect. Write "victims" for plural, more than one.

ABBREVIATIONS

The last subject we will cover is the use of abbreviations. This may fall under your individual departments policies and procedures, follow those first and foremost. For those agencies that are not specific, you can follow these guidelines and still be legally accurate.

The words that describe participants are long: complainant, defendant, witness, and so on. Accepted abbreviations for these long, easy to misspell words are: compl., def., witn,. Department policy overrules, but you will not be legally incorrect in using abbreviations. This goes for other words that are commonly abbreviated such as street, avenue, and boulevard, Mister and Mistress and Doctor.

St., Ave., Blvd., Mr., Mrs., Dr.

Abbreviations can be used around your department also.

Ofc., Cpl., Sgt., Lt., Capt., and on and on, especially if your spelling isn't so great.

Our department had a newly promoted Lieutenant that was eager to dive into his role and start placing useless memos on the roll call board for everyone to read. He came into roll call the next day to promote his ideas on personal and professional enrichment and asked how we had liked his memo.

He, to this day, has no idea why the room exploded in laughter. We told him the memo was a perfect example of him, at his best, and we expected many more like it. He had misspelled Lieutenant.

Chapter Five Privacy and Legal Issues

Sometimes in law enforcement we will have the opportunity to investigate offenses of a very serious and sensitive nature. When we write our police reports and complete the fill in the blank section there is usually some question from officers as to just how much information we are able to put on the front page.

Some agencies, when requested by the public for a police report, copy the front page only. Since most states have disclosure laws requiring the entire police report be given out to anyone that will pay the agency the copying fee, this is changing.

Currently, most states require a police agency to have a records custodian. The job of this records custodian is to determine what, if any, information on a police report is to be left confidential. The custodian will keep a file of restricted reports and have them marked accordingly with restricted victim and witness information blacked out. When any member of the public comes to the department requesting a copy of one of those restricted reports, they receive the entire report, but the restricted names and addresses are blacked out (Cerabino v. Bludworth). However, when a law enforcement officer or prosecutor requests a copy, the report is given to them in its entirety.

This is a very serious job for the records custodian. If the names of restricted victims and witnesses get out to the public, civil liability can fall on the agency and the records custodian personally.

RESTRICTED PEOPLE

Some of the restricted persons that are not open for disclosure are witnesses, for obvious reasons. Witnesses tied up with duct tape, residing in car trunks at the bottoms of rivers are very difficult to subpoena.

Victims of sexual assault, child abuse and children arrested for misdemeanor charges are also confidential.

When dealing with the subject of sex assault there are some tricky rules that make a report fully open to disclosure or keep portions of it confidential.

Victims of any type of sex assault, adult or juvenile are protected information. Unless the victim dies.

If the victim dies from alleged child abuse, their identity is not protected.

Remember all those news reports where the mother's new boyfriend was left to baby-sit the two-year-old and the two-year-old died of massive internal injuries to the abdomen? The picture of an adorable toddler is splashed across the news for all to see and grieve over. The next clip shows the mom hugging the child killer proclaiming her love for him regardless.

A fairly recent and sometimes controversial law, "Megan's Law," has forced law enforcement to disclose the identity of a person convicted of a sex offense.

Many years ago a little girl answered a knock at her front door. The person she met at the door was a neighbor. This neighbor sexually assaulted and murdered the child. Her name was Megan. Her family never knew a convicted Sexual Predator had moved in nearby and his appetite ran to little girls.

As a result of this tragic incident, legislation was enacted that says law enforcement "will" notify the public of the address and photograph of any and all convicted sex offenders in their immediate area.

Our department took this literally and officers enjoyed identifying the registered sexual offenders and sexual predators in our zones. One officer took it upon himself to notify an entire apartment complex of a certain registered sexual predators identity and location. The officer made up flyers with the sexual predators photo, name and apartment number on them. He put the flyers on every single car in the apartment complex. This sexual predator liked sneaking in unlocked sliding doors of sleeping women and beating and sexually assaulting them. This apartment complex was located next to a college and was predominantly filled with young women.

The sexual predator decided he should move. He moved into another apartment complex, near another college. The first officer notified the second officer and the second officer repeated the process. Bad guy decided to move again.

Last we heard he was living out in the middle of nowhere, in a broken down travel trailer. The deputy for the area knows who he is and reports the bad guy is living a very solitary lifestyle with a bunch of goats.

We received very minor criticism from fellow dirt bags. They decided the police were harassing the bad guy and his past was his past. The dirt bags said he did his time and should be left alone with his past kept secret. Because they liked him so much we suggested they allow him to move into their trailer park, since the bad guy was having so much trouble finding suitable living arrangements. We haven't heard from them since.

ARRESTS

When investigating a crime and a bad guy is arrested, all the information can be released to the public.

This includes the location, date, and time of the incident, a photo of the bad guy and details of the crime. However, if the release of this information may jeopardize the possibility of arresting a co-bad guy, then the information may be withheld.

The records custodian will not determine this. Since this information is specifically listed as public information and an arrest has been made, the decision to hold the information leading to the co-bad guy's arrest will come from the court. So, if you are working a hot case and the co-bad guy is waiting to run, get on the phone with your prosecutor's office immediately. The bad guy's attorney will be doing the same, beat them to the phone and to the judge.

The only exemptions in the release of arrested bad guys information is if the bad guy is a juvenile. Most states have now allowed the disclosure of a juvenile's arrest information if the crime is a felony. Crime details, school names, addresses and photos of the felony juvenile can be released. Be sure to check your own state laws regarding this to make sure every state has adopted the same legislation.

This is a double-edged sword. Kids involved in crimes severe enough may be profiled on the news. Photo, details, crying victims and all. This has been a phenomenal status symbol for gang kids, and kids that are just plain evil with no parental supervision.

If the juvenile in question is a particularly bad kid and they are being tried as an adult, then they fall under all the adult rules. If during the course of your investigation you are required to put together a photo pac or a line up, juvenile photos can be shown to victims and witnesses. Even if the additional juvenile's added to the line up are not suspects in this particular crime.

REALLY RESTRICTED PEOPLE

Officers and States' Attorneys, or prosecutors involved in any way in an offense are restricted (unless they get arrested). For the safety of the officer and his family, the home address, children's schools and spouse's work locations are restricted.

Undercover officers names and addresses are restricted from disclosure in any way. Making public the name and home address of an undercover officer is a misdemeanor in some states. Seeing how the media and police do not always see eye-to-eye, cops will prosecute for having their information made public every chance the media gives us.

Also in this area, the names and genders of confidential informants are restricted. Police officers get around this by giving the informant an identifying number, and leaving all the informant's information off the report. "C.I. number 42 advised..." identifies the informant in the report and the registered informants personal information is kept secret. Usually the complete file on the informant with a picture is kept in a secured area of the police department. The name remains confidential due to the fact the informant "could be harmed" (again with the car trunk scenario) and future investigations ruined by their identity being made public.

This is a very real threat. An informant that I had spoke with one day and paid for narcotics information, was killed the next day. The group of juveniles that he had just told me about, killed him. Apparently he bragged to them they were going to be arrested. They rewarded him by chasing him down the street, pushing him down and dropping a giant rock on his head.

Sometimes identifying an informant will go down to the wire in court. If a defense attorney insists on informant's name, and refuses a videotaped testimony, officers have been known to drop the case if the informant is especially good or if there are bigger and better cases on the horizon. (Ocala Star-Banner Corporation v. McGhee)

Another area in undercover work that should be left off of the report is the specifics on surveillance techniques and procedures. Saying generalized surveillance language such as, "I gave a non-verbal signal to my cover officer for the arrest team to move in." is enough. If the case goes to court and the defense attorney insists on the specifics being answered in open court, be ready for it. Say the information can jeopardize the safety of undercover officers and ruin investigations in the future if you disclose that information. Lean heavily on the safety issue, and future safety of officers. Now you have a judge sitting right there and a prosecutor ready to object to the line of questions. Most judges know what is going on and know the defense attorney has absolutely no need for specifics, and will rule in your favor.

When you go to discovery or a deposition prior to trial, every person in the room is allowed to hear privileged information. Let it all out. Both attorneys have unedited copies of the report and know everything anyway. Make the defense attorney understand that you have your case put together tightly, and their bad guy doesn't have a chance in court.

OFFICERS' RESPONSIBILITIES

What this means for the reporting officer, investigating and writing out the police report is nothing. We do not have to make any changes in how we fill out the police report, other than the areas we have covered. The investigation carries on as usual and the report is filled out as usual.

When writing out the narrative portion of the police report, every detail that you see fit to put in the report goes in. Nothing is confidential, or too personal.

Details on some reports may very well read like a horror novel or a pornographic book.

K.L.U.'S

Legally, police officers are able to put into a police report their conclusions. Documenting a conclusion is different than documenting an absolute.

As I mentioned previously, when a complainant tells you their version of what they think happened, or you come up with your own idea based on physical evidence at the scene, these are conclusions. Leave room for flexibility when writing about your investigative conclusions. Nothing is certain, everything is a possibility. Strange things happen at night, that sort of thing.

This area is also known, legally, as circumstantial. Movies always show the bad guy getting arrested for circumstantial evidence and facing the death penalty.

Real life does not allow this. The legal definition of Circumstantial Evidence is "...direct evidence as to facts deposed to but indirect as to the fatcum probandum...." Brown v. State.

"...inferences drawn from facts provided..." Hatfield v. Levy Bros.

"...existence of principal facts is only inferred from circumstances." Twin City Fire Ins. v. Lonas

What this all means in plain English is, a conclusion is an educated guess, based on the stuff left lying around by the bad guy.

Conclusions allow you to be flexible when a witness or other evidence is found that turns the investigation the other way. If you have documented your report as, *"this is what* **did** *happen based on my experience as a highly trained law enforcement officer blah, blah.....*" You have just locked yourself into a scenario. If you're wrong, you just gave the real bad guy an alibi, your official police report.

Absolutes, on the other hand, are certain, specific, with no room for argument. Such cases are those that you the police officer witness, or reliable witnesses, **with** physical evidence to match.

Be careful in writing an absolute. If you're right and you know you're right, defend your investigation vehemently. But if your case is based on a conclusion or is circumstantial in nature, remain flexible.

On the burglary call discussed earlier, we did not have a witness. We think the bad guy came in through the window, and walked out the front door. We have physical evidence that points to this. But we do not have a bad guy confessing or a witness stating this.

If you write on your police report, *"the defendant did enter through the south window and exited out the front door."* This is an absolute.

Sometime later a fat bad guy is caught. A year later in court, you show up to testify, and so does a mystery witness you never met. He was found by the defense attorney's investigator. Before you testify, the witness goes first and tells what he saw.

The mystery witness watched a fat bad guy break out the window, reach inside and open it. The fat bad guy put his hands on the windowsill and his foot on the side of the house and tried to pull himself in. He pulled, and jumped and kept falling down. The witness then watched the bad guy's skinny partner go around to the front, maybe to be a look out. The skinny bad guy walked right onto the front porch. The skinny bad guy looked around and stopped at the front door. He turned the knob and the door opened in his hand. The skinny bad guy went into the home. The fat bad guy, still trying to pull himself in, probably heard the skinny bad guy inside the house, thought it was the homeowner and ran off.

Here is what will happen to you, on the stand. You will describe the crime scene and talk about how the suspect climbed in the window and took the complainant's stuff. Then the bad guy walked out the front door. You will be asked about the possibility of a second bad guy. You saw no indications of a second bad guy, so you will answer no. The jury will be very amused at this point. You will have no idea why and the defense attorney won't let you in on the joke. Your prosecutor will be kicking himself under the table for not telling you to remain non-specific. Guess who might get to go free!!

A way to alleviate this from ever happening is to remain non-specific on an unknown.

When there is not a witness, no arrest and only physical evidence, remain flexible.

Write the point of entry, the window, as the **possible** point of entry and **possible** point of exit. This will be based on your experience, the physical evidence present at the scene and a lack of corroborating testimony.

Then later, when this mystery witness arrives you can honestly testify to only the absolutes of: footprints on the wall, broken window, smeared fingerprints on the sill and an open front door. Was there the possibility of the second bad guy being involved? Of course. If the defense attorney tries to pin you down to an absolute, stick to the physical evidence as being your only evidence of anything happening at all.

After a couple of minutes of the defense attorney badgering the poor officer on the stand, you will come out looking as if you tried to give all the information you could, based on the facts you had at the time. Appearing as if you did not know it all and knowing when to say," I don't know," makes you look humble to the jury. The last thing the jury wants to see is a know it all officer who's theory was just proven wrong by the previous witness.

DOCUMENTING INJURIES

Remaining flexible is also extremely important in describing injuries. If you have an injury investigation and you have an interview from a victim, describing injuries is fine. However this changes if the person is dead.

During a death investigation you will probably have found out circumstances leading up to the injuries on the body. Be careful when you look at a hole in someone, and try to write about it. If you are not a pathologist, do not say what the person died from. Do not describe the trauma on a dead person as a bullet wound from a small caliber pistol. If the trauma turns out to be a hole from a screwdriver, stabbed into the victim, you have just created a conflict that the medical examiner has to try to compensate for.

Describe only what you see. Describe the hole, approximate dimensions, where it is and leave it at that. The same with what may appear to be severe bruising on a body.

Lividity occurs when the blood pools in the lowest extremities and lowest portions of the body, after death. Don't describe this as horrific bruising on the body and proclaim the 87-year-old natural death a brutal homicide.

You are always better off in death investigations in leaving the conclusions to the experts. The detectives and pathologists and coroners come in after you do.

Medical Examiners need to know the circumstances leading up to the death of a person so they can form their own conclusions. Don't make it harder for them by putting your own conclusions in writing.

They are the highly trained professionals and will decide what really happened here, thank you very much!

Chapter Six
Arrest Affidavits

The ultimate goal in law enforcement is to govern over a society of lawful, peaceful people. People come and go without ever having the oppressing thoughts of random criminal acts to destroy the utopia of their existence.

Let's hope not. Lots of bad guys teaching up and coming bad guys how to do bad things is job security.

Throughout your career in law enforcement, you will be rewarded for all your hard work of investigating crimes, interviewing witnesses, with the ultimate arrest of bad guys. Your investigations will be flawless, reports detailed and articulately written, arrests uneventful, and the court proceedings smooth. Yes, with the properly written report, this can really happen!

We have gone over in detail, what is needed to write that flawless, articulate, detailed report. It will be so spectacular; the only thing the defense attorney will have to attack is the signature on the affidavit cannot be read clearly. The attorney will sweat in his cheap linen suit, causing wrinkles to sprout up in the most unbecoming places, only visible when he walks away from the jury to wipe his sweaty forehead.

When you gain experience in a particular area, such as narcotics, undercover work, car thefts or any other area that interests you, you will learn something new each time you go to court on an arrest. Defense attorneys will pull all the tricks out of their bag on the first case to try to win.

What this does for us is lay out everything they know. They give us their secrets, defense styles, and let us know what amount of prep work they typically do.

I worked for several years on an undercover squad. During my three years I made over 700 arrests for prostitution and drug related charges. My cases became so streamlined, I developed a solid and articulate habit in note taking and report writing.

Each time I went to court and lost, I found out why. Learned from that and made the adjustment so this detail was covered the next time. You can only screw up these types of simple cases so many times. After my first initial cases were dumped, nolle prosequi, or found not guilty, I asked why. Attorneys were more than happy to tell the judge in open court that I had failed to write this in, document that detail, statute number was one number off, or certain detail left unexplained and so on. This was great free legal advice.

When the kinks were worked out, and the arrest teams and processing teams began to work smoothly, I soon had a conviction rate of over 98%.

I never could have done it without the humiliation delved out to me by the repeated remarks of my incompetent investigations, discovered by clever defense attorneys.

Unfortunately this will happen to you too, or probably already has. How to complete the interviews and work on the investigation has already been covered. When you are out there working on the street and you manage to catch that first bad guy, there are two things you can do to him.

NOTICE TO APPEAR

First, if your state allows it and the crime is a misdemeanor, he can be released with the promise to appear in court. The bad guy has to sign a piece of paper saying he promises to show up and then we let him go. Each state and each agency has rules that vary for this procedure, known as ROR. Release on Recognizance.

CUFF 'N' STUFF

The second thing that you can do to the bad guy is make a physical arrest. This means handcuff the bad guy and take him / her to jail, also known as "cuff-n-stuff."

In order to get the bad guy in jail, he will need his "get into jail" pass. This get into jail pass is called an affidavit. Arrest affidavit, probable cause affidavit, criminal report affidavit and many other names, agency to agency.

This affidavit will usually be specific to the county where you work. The county sheriff runs most jails. The county sheriff allows all agencies, located within his county, to bring their bad guys to him. The bad guy gets arrested by municipal, airport, or reservation police and ultimately ends up in jail for the county the offense was committed in.

When the bad guy gets his case processed, it goes through the court system, by the same county's state prosecutor's office. The prosecutor's office works very closely with law enforcement and is on the officer's side when the time comes to go to court. This prosecutor's office is usually responsible for the creation of the affidavit that will be used by all law enforcement agencies within their county. The prosecutor will make the affidavit available to all agencies and allows agency input in the creation of the document.

The affidavit you see and use will be shared by several different agencies. It is very important that you understand how this document is filled out. It looks like a simple fill in the blank style report, with a narrative at the bottom. It might be carboned with many copies so it can be separated and the copies can be routed to the interested parties.

WHAT GOES HERE?

As a result of this multi-jurisdictional-multi-task-multi-bad guy-for-any crime-juvenile-adult-felony or-misdemeanor-document, there are going to be some spaces on the affidavit you will not need to complete.

Carry a spare, original affidavit in your notes. On this original affidavit have the blanks filled out properly, or a description of what goes in them. The blanks that need to be left empty need to be marked in a way so you understand that they can be left blank or lined through. That way, late at night when you are exhausted after a foot chase, a fence climbing and a fight to get the cuffs on, you won't have to think too much. You may spend unnecessary time looking up, in a procedures manual, what goes in that one little tiny blank, only to discover, for your agency, nothing does.

This fill in the blank area is usually very simple. Name of the bad guy with all his personal information, almost identical to what we practiced collecting in previous chapters, needs to be written down.

When filling in the blanks, be as complete as possible. This document is the first to go to the jail and the first to appear in morning court with the prosecutor and judge. Everything you put on this affidavit gets entered into a permanent database within the jail. This database is eagerly shared nationwide and agency wide, including federal agencies. Lots of bad guys have been caught because an arrest affidavit had a bad guy's former address, in another state, in a database in some tiny, Nowhereville county.

If your bad guy has had a case of amnesia and has forgotten his name, or the bad girl has decided she does not want you to have it, there is a name you can give them, for charging purposes.

John and Jane Doe. These are fictitious names that are given to parties in legal proceedings until their real identity is discovered. (State v. Rossignol)

Some bad guys are particularly resistant and won't even give you their address. Under this area you can put, "*at large*." This means, "not restrained to any particular area." Well, except for one area, guess who is not getting out of jail until they can remember who they are and where they belong?

When filling out the charging area of the affidavit you will have state statutes and enforcement codes that you will need to use. Fill in the appropriate code, usually with the crime written out. This is an area where clever abbreviations are not appreciated. Such as Burglary P.T. In our state this is burglary with petit theft, misdemeanor theft. P.T. needs to be written out to avoid confusion and possibly allowing a bad guy to be charged with the wrong crime. You know what happens then?? Back to Latin "nolle prosequi," case dropped.

Some counties need evidence filled in; spaces are on the affidavit for this also. Just a note to remember. This is not the primary documentation for the chain of custody of evidence. Always write out the complete chain of custody on the police report.

WHAT DID HE DO?

When you have filled in all the blanks on the affidavit, you will have come across the narrative. This area is the lined area at the bottom and will have something that reads, "state facts to establish probable cause a crime was committed." What this means is, what did the bad guy do?

I've watched many officers struggle with this particular area. Either too much or too little detail is put in. Keep in mind on this same piece of paper, just a few inches above the narrative, is date, time, locations and names. Don't repeat any of this information.

Keep the probable cause simple. Remember the synopsis area of the main police report, we needed the elements for the statute? This area is asking for the same information. Document that the elements were met, but not necessarily how. Details of how is what the police report is for.

Using the burglary we have been referring to for this entire book, pretend we did chase down the bad guy, that ran out the front door, and we caught him.

- The affidavit needs the elements for the crime of burglary, and any secondary, or attempted secondary crime. Starting off with a standard statement to get you moving, put on the affidavit:

Generic Arrest Affidavit

The defendant did

This forces us to get right to the point. Keep that brief format idea in mind, don't repeat any information from the top and justify the first crime. Remember chronological order.

Generic Arrest Affidavit

The defendant did **enter the complainants home,**
without permission and took the listed items.

Again keeping it brief, what was the secondary crime, necessary in a burglary?

Listed items are "stuff" that was taken. It will be itemized on the police report, no need to have it here, again, clogging up the affidavit.

- The next area on this narrative that needs to be completed is the identity section. This can be a separate section or incorporated into one big narrative. What this part of the narrative is asking you for is to identify the defendant as the person who committed the crime.

For the purposes of an **on scene** arrest that you witness, this is simple.

"I observed the defendant commit the above offenses."

Not too much to argue with there. Your name will be on the affidavit in an assigned space. You may also legally call yourself the Affiant. This is personal preference, and a habit for some. But, just a simple, "I did this..." works just as well.

If we arrived late to the scene and were met by witnesses who gave us the bad guys description and location, we would be making a probable cause arrest. However, it is not written any differently in the narrative. "The defendant did..." is all the same. The second part where we identify the suspect will be different.

By law you cannot catch a bad guy and take him back to the scene without his permission. If we caught this bad guy 6 blocks away and the witness says "I can recognize him if I see him again." Move the witness to the bad guy. We are allowed to detain the bad guy. Have the witness tell an officer either a definite yes, or no, as the witness is driven by the bad guy. Try to keep the witness concealed, if at all possible, remember the car trunk?

If the identification is yes, arrest your bad guy. In filling out the affidavit for the second part simply write...

Generic Arrest Affidavit

The defendant did enter the complainants home,
without permission and took the listed items.
The defendant was identified, by the witness as the
person who committed the above crime.

For probable cause arrests you will have witnesses or victims or complainants. List them by role, just like in the police report, on the narrative portion of the affidavit. Their name and personal information will be on the upper part of the affidavit and also on the police report.

For the final part of the affidavit we need to know how we got the bad guy's name. If he is carrying identification, so much the better.

Generic Arrest Affidavit

The defendant did enter the complainants home,
without permission and took the listed items. The
defendant was identified, by the witness as the person
who committed the above crime. **The defendant**
identified himself with a valid Dept. of Corrections
I.D. card.

Or

The defendant identified himself verbally.

Or

The defendant refused to identify himself. (John Doe will learn to love jail food, and his roommate Bubbah)

If we are writing out an affidavit for a probable cause arrest and the bad guy is not there, but the victim or witness knows the bad guy's name, how do they know?

The victim identified the defendant as the person who committed this offense.

And

The victim is a relative and knows the defendant by name.

Or

The victim used to work with the defendant and knows him by name.

If your victim appears to be picking a name out of the air or something just does not seem right, do some more investigating on the identity of the bad guy. Arresting the wrong person, even though the victim named him, can still cost you money.

The affidavit becomes part of public record, and part of the permanent report. It is available to the public, but usually has a marked out section for the witness and victim information to be kept confidential by obscuring the carbon. It is the first document in the charging process and is read the most.

Remember, keep them simple, elements for the crime must be there but not the exact details.

When you are finished with the affidavit and are ready to take the bad guy to jail, the affidavit may need to be notarized.

Some states allow a certified law enforcement officer to act as a witness on a signature for an official affidavit. What this means is you can act as the official witness on an affidavit and sign it in lieu of a notary.

However, this does not mean that because you are a cop, you are now automatically a notary. Don’t put a sign in your front yard, and don’t start marrying people.

This is just for official “cop” related affidavits only.

The witnessing of the signature also gives law enforcement a “checks and balances” where the affidavit, the arrest, has to be approved by someone else.

I can tell you from experience, supervisors do not like to be told at the end of the shift that you arrested a murder suspect when they did not know anything about it.

Chapter Seven Use of Force Documentation

Unfortunately, there will be times in your career that you will meet up with some people that just don't like the police. These people will have varying reasons for not liking you, ranging from treatment from previous arrests to televisions portrayal of you.

You will be yelled at, cursed at, spit on, stepped on, punched and possibly even shot. Try not to take this personally. Police officers are, in my experience, some of the finest people in the world, to each other. We don't like bad guys and bad guys don't like us. As long as we all understand this, things seem to go fairly well.

However, you will, at some point meet that small percentage of over-intoxicated, sweat-stained, broken down pick-up truck driving, gator-wrestling bad guy. When you show up at their place you may have been invited, or you may not. If you had to respond back into the swamps to their 1960's single wide, mildew- stained, aluminum family abode to discuss the rules governing spouse discipline, you might meet one of them.

If you respond to just such a call and encounter the family wage earner, who tells you, between spits of chewing tobacco, that police are not needed, but his common law 15-year-old wife is screaming, “help me! help me!,” from inside, a sound that is slightly muffled by aluminum and paneling. You’re there.

After conducting a thorough investigation, remember two sides to every story, and you have come to the determination that the bad guy must go to jail, arrest him. If this bad guy just happens to be one of those that does not want to go to jail “again” and thinks they can get away from you, they might try to do it.

The vast majority of bad guys that are arrested and end up in a fight or a resist with a police officer, are trying to get away from you. Remember “Fight or Flight”? Most are flight. If they are one of the fight types and you have managed to utter those fateful words, “you are under arrest” and get a hand on them, watch out.

TV and movies show the police officer in a hand-to-hand, standing fistfight with the bad guy. The fight lasts for several minutes with each delivering punches to the other.

In a real fight with a bad guy you will end up on the ground. It will always be in a mud hole and you will roll a lot. Your main objective will be to get the bad guys hands secured in handcuffs. There are usually not a lot of punches thrown except by the police. And we are definitely the only ones to show up with an expandable or other police baton. Even though we get hit the most by them.

If the fight lasts especially long and you get tired, you may need to escalate your use of force, actions taken, and weapons used to keep the upper hand in this fight. You may need several officers to assist you, each using their own perceived level of force. When the bad guy is finally restrained and secured, you can get out from under the bottom of the pile and dust yourself off.

The decision that causes an officer to use force is determined solely by the bad guy.

Police do not get to decide upon arrival at the single wide that this is going to be an OC arrest. It is up to the bad guy and his actions.

When you have been forced to resort to the use of force to effect an arrest, you will need to remember what your actions were, and why, for documentation. The documentation that you complete can save you from administrative and civil action.

Police officers are highly trained in defensive tactics. We get trained in the academy and further that training with updates, classes and seminars on the subject. The officer's reactions to situations, created and forced upon you by your bad guy, is placed and ranked on a scale. This scale, used almost universally, is called a Confrontation Continuum. The Confrontational Continuum also includes side notes used to determine when an officer may escalate or de-escalate the use of force based on environmental factors. I'm not talking about fighting in the high winds of a hurricane but, such environmental factors as age, strength, ability, location, fatigue and size of not just yourself but the bad guy too, just to name a few.

First and foremost is presence (Command presence). Just showing up dressed like a cop may calm, and control. If you happen to be large and mean looking this is easy. Merely showing up is a use of force. Just by arriving in a marked car, and being in a police uniform can alter the outcome of the event you have arrived at. You are there but you have not been forced to do anything yet.

However, if you show up in full riot gear because you think something may happen, that will be considered a show of force, completely different, but still the same.

Dialogue is taught in the academy and gained through experience, as an officer's ability to control a scene by words alone. If you have a calm voice and a quick mind and are able to direct and organize, dialogue can be all that is needed.

When dialogue is not enough and the bad guy forces you to escalate in order to control a situation, there are several variables to consider. First, if this bad guy really doesn't want to go to jail, can you physically put him there? If the answer is no, why not? Is he too big, are you too little, are you tired, is he standing in front of you wearing white wrap around pajamas, held up by a wide black belt!? Does he have a weapon? Does he have an item that appears to be a weapon? Are you fighting in a dangerous place, like the side of the interstate during a traffic stop? Is he an escaped murder suspect with nothing to loose?

Your department will teach you how to respond to all the above variables. You will know your department's use of force, deadly force and pursuit policies, by heart, and follow them to the letter. Also be aware of the state laws governing your actions in use of force. Some state and federal laws allow police to commit certain acts of violence under the color of law, and if done properly with the correct intent, protect the officer from criminal charges. Agency's will write out their own policies and contradict some of those laws. Make sure you follow agency rules, you might not get arrested, but you will get fired.

Using force to control a situation or affect an arrest is your job, and it's okay to do your job. You are expected to protect others and defend yourself. You are expected to arrest bad guys and you are expected to go home to your children each and every night. The use of force is authorized, legal and is inevitable of a police officer doing their job right.

Everyone may not understand why you chose to use a certain measure of force, and we don't have to explain it to all of him or her, but we do have to document why we used that level of force on a police report.

Proper, precise, thorough documentation in use of force situations will save you, time and time again. Administratively and civilly. If you do not explain why you did what you did, including environmental factors that influenced your decision, a person reviewing a bad guys use of force complaint may be forced to believe a bad guy's complaint story first, remember the "first story lesson" from the previous chapter? Your reiterated account later may sound as if you are embellishing, or adding to cover up your actions. Even when you are totally in the right.

WHERE TO BEGIN

Write your story under the actions taken area of the Investigation.

Create a mental picture and walk us through. Be a storyteller and use adjectives. Be humble, and don't be afraid to document you were scared, sometimes, to death.

Make sure your narrative, detailing a use of force incident is written just like you would write out any other report. Chronological order, from the beginning, all the way to the end result.

WHAT TO SAY AND HOW TO SAY IT

You will be familiar with your agency's terminology for certain specific actions you take. Such as strikes, kicks, and escort techniques. You will know the names of all your weapons and equipment. When describing these various items, do not abbreviate. If you used pepper spray, use its proper name, *Oleoresin Capsicum*. Using the proper technical names of defensive tactics techniques, weapons and equipment makes your report look professional, complete and in control. Use "calm" words to describe actions you had to take. Words such as deploy, strike and deliver in place of beat, and knee-blast. Stay away from any words that sound like bashing, smashing, crashing, blasting, breaking, cracking or snapping.

Talk about the techniques you used and why you felt you were forced to use them. When you escalated your use of force document what was happening to you. Did you already deploy a certain technique, only to have the bad guy look at you and laugh? Was he a 400-pound professional wrestler, mad and intoxicated, threatening to choke slam you? Where was your back up?

If you respond to this call to assist as back up and you are forced, along with the other eleven officers it takes to handcuff the bad guy, write out your actions. Document what information **you** had about the call prior to your arrival. What did **you** see on your arrival and why did **you** need to use force? What techniques did **you** use, and were they effective?

Use chronological order, just like in all other reports. Don't depend on the originating officer, the first one on the scene, to document your actions for you. They have enough to worry about with their own documentation and may not even know you were there, somewhere in the pile of bodies.

If your agency has a check the block form for use of force and it seems fairly specific, complete that but also document the fight in narrative format.

Again, the investigation is your opportunity to tell the story of how you saw the call. You are allowed to write out your fears, concerns and thoughts in this area. They are your fears and concerns and you are never wrong. No one can tell you how you should have reacted, and they will try, especially in a shooting. But remember you were there, they were not.

Document your fears and what you **thought** was going to happen. What you thought was going to happen is legally enough for you to react. You don't have to wait for the bad guy pointing the gun at you to fire first, to defend yourself!

When you are in a simple fight that causes you to use force on a bad guy, and the situation escalates, remember why. Don't document, "the hairs stood up on the back of your neck so you fired your gun at the bad guy;" you'll end up in jail. Document that the bad guy made gestures, movements, you saw, you knew, you heard, or your intent was.

INTENT

Intent is another important element to remember here. Training in a defensive tactics class is done under very strict, controlled conditions. The bad guy, your partner, is usually a "yes" person, standing still waiting for you to whale on them with your kicks and punches.

Real bad guys react a little differently. First they simply will not hold still and let you hit them again and again with your expandable baton. They wiggle when they see the canister of OC spray come out of your belt, and they duck when you try to shoot them.

Sometimes things just don't always go like they were supposed to, like in class. It's the bad guys extra, unanticipated movement that frequently gets them hurt.

During an arrest of a burglary suspect I hit him in the head with my expandable baton. This could be considered a use of deadly force. I had no right to use deadly force. Why did I hit him in the head? I didn't mean to, it was never my intent. But, I didn't have any difficulty explaining myself because of my initial intent.

Here is what the scene looked like. A fourteen-year-old black male was hit in the head, with an expandable baton by a white officer, the child was knocked unconscious. The child was unarmed.

Remember the "first story" rule? Your supervisor arriving on the scene may not get to you first. The crowd growing to watch the arrest and action will repeat the first story they hear. The above synopsis sounds bad for the police. This is a good story for the crowd to repeat.

Later you will have to come in and clarify all this. The benefit is you will do it on paper, in a cool, concise manner using technical jargon to describe the precision techniques you were forced to deploy on the subject in an attempt to gain compliance so you could affect an arrest.

Here is what happened:

> *The bad guy was seen entering a residence through an open window. On my arrival I found his bicycle propped up under the open window, and I could hear him moving around inside. My back up arrived and we surrounded the house. Bad guy came out. I caught him as he tried to drop to the ground. He was sweaty and slipped completely out of my grasp. He ran and I chased. We ran to a fence, he climbed. I yelled for an officer that was trying to cut him off, to tackle the bad guy. The officer tried but the bad guy's momentum pulled them both over the fence. They flopped and rolled as they fell. Bad guy ended up on the top of the heap of bodies. I was trying to come over the fence when I saw the bad guy raise his hand. His hand was in a fist and he was looking straight down at the officer he was sitting on top of.*

Here is how the police report read:

> *"I was afraid the suspect was going to punch the officer in the face. I extended my ASP baton and attempted to deliver a single strike to the defendant's left forearm, in an attempt to stop the defendant from striking and injuring another officer. The defendant suddenly, and unexpectedly, lifted his arm out of my reach and I missed his forearm. I struck the defendant on the left side of his head. This caused the defendant to become immediately unconscious and created a small raised bump on the side of his head with a small cut approximately a half-inch wide. The defendant was placed into handcuffs without further incident."*

The defendant, after he became conscious, told me all he was trying to do was reach up to grab the fence behind him so he could pull himself off the officer and run away.

I had no way of knowing this. My intent was to stop the defendant from harming another officer. My use of force was completely justified, I was not required to wait until the bad guy hit the officer to prove his actions before I could react, and I didn't. I was completely honest, and relayed my fears in detail to the officer on the ground and to my supervisor at the scene.

If I had assumed I was going to get into trouble for this action, or I could somehow make it look better by embellishing, it would be a lie. Lies are not necessary. Everyone makes mistakes, just be able to explain why you did what you did.

Always document all uses of force, no matter how minor. Don't be lulled into thinking that a simple resist where you had to wrench up the bad guy's hand, and heard a funny popping noise, does not need to be documented. That bad guy will be the surgeon in training that can no longer work with his hands.

ASSISTING THE WOUNDED

After you are finished fighting the bad guy and you were forced to use any of your weapons on him, he may need medical attention. If he does not need medical attention but needs assistance, document how you helped him. Spraying someone with pepper spray is an escalation in use of force. Getting sprayed with pepper spray is an excruciating experience. For the bad guy and all the officers receiving over spray. When a bad guy gets sprayed, the oily residue will be concentrated, probably in his face. All the mucus membranes will be at their height of aggravation and he will be in pain. The oil must be dried before the bad guy can be transported, so the transporting officer does not get contaminated too. To speed up the drying some officers use a fan, the vent from the car and some officers even carry the long life shelf milk in a carton. The enzymes in the milk stop the burning, so they say. Any measures you use to aid or comfort the bad guy should be documented in the report. This action will make you look like a conscientious police officer doing his job. This looks great to the jury, months down the road, even though you would probably rather have splashed water on his face to reactivate, just to see if he would do that dance again.

The same goes for any other type of a use of force in which there are injuries or perceived injuries. Call an ambulance to the scene. Document the ambulance company, unit number, names of the drivers and any other emergency personnel. If the bad guy has to be taken to the hospital, treatment you personally did at the scene along with hospital personnel's treatment needs to be documented.

TAPED DOCUMENTATION

Probably the worst situation a law enforcement officer can be involved in is to be forced to use deadly force against another human being. If you have been forced to escalate to this extreme level of force it is probably because your, or another's life was threatened. This is when things go bad. All the jokes police tell about pucker factors and the criticism we give another about tunnel vision, all combine to create the most dynamic, terrifying, exhilarating experience in law enforcement. Then everything stops.

All you are required to do at this point is tell us what happened. You will need to remember the actions leading up to the deadly force, mitigating circumstances, environmental factors influencing your decision to shoot and the exact details both before and after the shell casings drop. Hopefully your department will see you as the victim and you will be interviewed. Someone else will write out your report treating you just like you would treat a victim involved in a shooting. The only difference here is your interview will probably be conducted on tape. The tape will be transcribed with every "uumm," "like," "sort a" spelled out in illiterate detail.

Before you go into this type of interview, take several moments to compose yourself. Find a place to relax so you can organize your thoughts. Briefly read over your department's deadly force or shooting policies, just to reaffirm your actions were right on line. But to also make sure you will be using exact terminology, as is listed in the policy manuals. What these few minutes of quiet time will do is allow you to almost remove yourself from the situation. Keeping it from becoming an intensely personal situation and turning it into what it is, a highly dynamic, volatile act in which you were forced to defend yourself or another from being killed. It will also allow you a few minutes to read up so you will be able to get technical when you need to.

This interview, being on tape will need to be the best interview you have ever given. Do not conduct the interview until you feel you are thinking clearly and can explain your actions in great detail using correct terminology. Just like you do when you testify in court, speak clearly and if you do not understand a question have it repeated or rephrased. Don't allow someone to pressure you into agreeing on what your actions were or insist your perceptions were wrong. Above all, if for any reason the room gets too hot or if you are uncomfortable, use an old interview technique to your own advantage ... take a break. If you are feeling threatened or intimidated or just plain old awful about what happened and you want someone on your side, get an attorney. Even if you know you have not done anything wrong.

Ultimately appearing on paper as the cool, calm and in control officer attempting to effect an arrest by using proper use of force techniques delivered for specific reasons, determined by the reactions of the bad guy, and causing unfortunate and possibly debilitating injuries, due to his lack of cooperation, is our goal here.

The fact that you were really a sweating, wind sucking police officer, screaming for back up on your radio, sounding like a girl, flailing wildly with your baton, is irrelevant.

Chapter Eight Computer Report Writing

Since the beginning of law enforcement, officers have recorded events of crime fighting, heroism, self-less bravery, and downright idiocy. These events have been documented laboriously by hand, onto paper, and stuck into a file. Not much has changed over the years.

Law enforcement equipment is now available that is the cutting edge of technology. Every department has those few officers who, with their own money go out and buy the latest and greatest gadgets. These Star Trek wanna-bees show up to your calls loaded down with so much confusing, shiny black plastic, technological looking stuff, the rear bumper on their car almost drags the ground.

For the average department, dollars are not available to have this marvelous stuff purchased and issued to everyone. If your department is particularly small, and your area has a decent tax base then you may work for one of these lucky agencies that get new cars fully loaded, with all the best.

Good grant writers are also responsible for acquiring very available money that can be spent on police goodies.

But, for those of us that work for larger metropolitan cities, with no decent grant writer, and lots of crashed cars from pursuits, expensive toys are an unattainable commodity.

One of the favorite, but pricey pieces of equipment that police officers like and use the most is the addition of a mobile computer, mounted into the police car.

Computers allow the officers to receive calls for service. Surf through and select calls they want to take, and ignore all calls they don't want like calls that involve flies on windows with funny smells and missing neighbors. Computers also allow officers and supervisors to monitor each other's activities, duration of call and current location. E-mail saves radio air time and allows quick messages from the dispatcher to the individual unit. It also allows officer safety messages to be sent to every available unit that is logged on. Some safety messages even beep and will not go away until the officer acknowledges and deletes it.

We can run our bad guy's name in the quiet privacy of our car and receive information about warrants and stolen cars.

Computers in the police car are also being used to write police reports. Incident reports can be quickly and neatly written. Depending on the program, spell check can be used and the report transmitted to the supervisor for editing. The report can also be saved on a standard floppy disc and taken into the station at the end of the shift and downloaded, edited and printed out. Some programs allow the officers to send the report directly to the main station for processing. Still some programs allow the officer to write the probable cause affidavit, for their bad guy that has been arrested, and have it transmitted directly to the jail for receiving.

The computer of choice for this application is of course the laptop computer. These are not your everyday, home or office laptop's but a sturdy, waterproof, coffee proof, shock resistant, pursuit resistant model.

This computer is usually mounted in the car, over the center console or the passenger knee space on a sharp, hard metal arm. Due to the anticipated driving habits of the police officer, the computer is mounted in a stationary position. It cannot be moved or swivelled, once in position, except by the use of power tools, grease and skinned knuckles.

As a result of this lack of flexibility in positioning the computer, there have been several complaints by officers against using computers for report writing.

For any officer over, about 5', 9" in height, that has been assigned to one of the smaller police cars, it gets crowded quickly. Next to the officer's knees there is a police radio, siren control, light bar control, microphone for a PA system and the radio in addition to the computer console. If you are the passenger in this car you will have the computer resting on your left knee. You can forget about getting into the glove box and the ashtray will never be seen again.

The position that the officer must sit in to reach the computer keyboard twists the officer's back. Carpal tunnel flourishes, as the officer has no hand rest available, the bucket seats catch the officer's gun belt and the screen causes temporary blindness for those working nights. If the officer is heavy (or fat) the wedge created by the officer's arm reaching across the steering wheel to type, can probably get pretty uncomfortable.

However, on the pro side for using the computer for report writing, officers are usually more thorough when typing and tend to add more detail. This is always beneficial to the case when more explicit detail is added. Spelling and grammar checks are built in to most programs. The need to add detail to the report after it is edited, reread and proofread is as easy as typing it in to the appropriate place on the report. Cut and paste areas of the narrative can be shifted around as needed. Some programs will allow you to incorporate a wants and warrants check, from your records or warrants division, directly into the body of the report, without retyping.

Depending on the speed of the typist, two-finger pecker or the speed queen, the computer can produce a detailed report much faster than hand writing can.

Typed reports are always neater than the handwritten product and the printed report looks very professional.

There are several computer programs available within the police world that assists officers in writing neat, complete reports on a laptop.

Most of the report programs that were researched have a similar on-screen report appearance to the paper variety. They have the various fields for data entry that can be moved to and from with either the Tab or the mouse. Some even have that little arrow with the fall down menu to choose the offense, location and suspect information, among others.

These on-screen reports have a synopsis and a narrative area, just like we reviewed in the first part of this book. Unfortunately, modern technology can only go so far in writing police reports. The computer report form still has that big, blank narrative section that will need to be typed out, in its entirety, by you, by hand. The best part is you no longer need "Rookie Juice." The big blank narrative is the same as the paper variety that we already discussed. You will write in "Investigation" and "Interview" just as you did on paper, but with all the benefits of the word processor.

Many software companies have realized what an untapped market police report writing programs can fill. A few companies have tried to supplement the police report writing market with their own product. As a result, some companies have targeted the smaller police agency, and still others are accommodating the larger agencies.

One of my favorites, for a small agency, is a program that was developed by two full-time police officers from St. Louis, Missouri. Robert Muffler and Richard Will have created a program that is complete, and user friendly. Their company, Automated Police Systems, Inc. created a report writing program called, Automated Law Enforcement Incident Report (A.L.E.I.R.).

Any agency, or individual officer can purchase the software, in components as needed. Different, individual components include, the incident report, supplement report, non-criminal incident report, arrest report, traffic accident report and notice to appear for the state of Florida, just to name a few. These reports can be loaded into network or laptop computers for a car, remote location, distant office or even the officer's home. The completed reports information is stored on a 3.5" disk and uploaded into the department's database and network when convenient.

This software package is a complete *Windows* based computerized police records management system. It combines word processing and data processing that is actually affordable. The programs are customizable to the individual agency.

The program is priced at a very moderate $300.00 for each component. You must purchase the Incident Report software first, then purchase the supplemental software as needed. The price licenses any agency to install and use the programs on as many computers as needed, as long as the software is used by your agency only.

Agencies purchasing the basic program will receive updates to the program for two years. You can download the software for a free 30-day trial run, for free!

To contact these soon to be millionaire's and take a look at their software and great WEB site; Automated Police Systems Inc.

5231 Jamieson
St. Louis Missouri 63109 (314) 752-9995
www.aleir.com Email info@aleir.com

For the larger agencies that need software that will be multi-functional and have the ability to expand, but still be affordable for licensing to multiple computers, here is a great product.

VersaTerm, a computer program developed by a Canadian company is available, customizable and easy to use. The program is a complete Linux based, records management system, but works like *Windows*. It can be used to create databases to convert old information into the new system that makes the information available to anyone on the network.

The police program, called Versadex, can be customized to each agency's needs. Report writing can be completed on the car's laptop and within the police building, via the network. Within the building, non-emergency reporting officers use the simple system, write complete reports and transmit them to the supervisor for editing. The report is then transmitted to records for storage, completely paperless!

When writing reports, the street officer can use a simple fill in the blank and narrative report, add any comments needed, and ship the report to the supervisor for editing. If additions or changes need to be made the report is transmitted back to the officer, with instructions, and changes made.

The officer can complete a records check from several types of databases within the station. If the report seems similar to a recent event, or the officer wants previous reports from the address, an incident search can be done from the car. Cut and clip from these various databases can be accomplished, with the retrieved information added to the report simply and quickly.

This program also allows e-mail to be sent along with messaging. Of course spell check is available to make the report look professional and read well.

The only negative feedback I was able to find about the Versadex system was the printed appearance. While on the computer screen, the fields that need to be filled in, appear neat and organized. However, the completed, printed report is not. The printed product appears in a plain, typewriter style font. There are no lines or headings to direct the eye and the overall appearance is somewhat amateurish, making it difficult to find what you are looking for. Unfortunately, this finished appearance takes away from what we are trying to accomplish, by typing reports, anyway. I understand I am not the only person that noticed this problem, a new format can be created by using templates, customized to your agency.

One of the best features of this program is the technical support. After installation, a technical advisor stays near the agency and trains, troubleshoots, and repairs any problems that may arise. After that tech person has left, phone in tech support has never been more than 30 minutes away. E-mail conferences are always available, if the problem does not involve a complete system crash.

To contact this company:	Versaterm Inc.
Address:	2300 Carling Ave. Ottawa, Ontario, Canada K2B 7G1
Phone Number:	(613) 820-0311
Fax	(613) 596-5884
E-mail	info@versaterm.com
Web Site:	www.versaterm.com

As far as that positional problem with the officer sitting in the car twisting to type on the keyboard, Texas Industrial Peripherals has a solution.

This company has developed a keyboard that connects to the car's laptop computer. This keyboard is approximately the same size as the keyboard on the laptop. It comes with a custom made power cord so the officer, either the passenger or the driver, can stretch the keyboard to where ever they need it, get comfortable and type.

If you work evenings or midnights the keyboard even comes equipped with keys that have letters and numbers that glow in the dark. The keyboard is sealed against leaks and is fairly sturdy, for those emergency starts and stops. A built in mouse is on the keyboard along with an emergency key.

This little goodie is priced at almost $400.00, but! They get cheaper the more you buy. The cables can be cut to almost any length you may need. To contact this company, Texas Industrial Peripherals SL-86-911. 1800-866-6506. Or www.ikey.com.

These are only a few of the programs available. Some promise great advances for police agencies in report writing, and some others really try to simplify the officer's hot, hectic day.

When looking into police report writing programs for your agency, search for a company that, at least, has police involved in the production of the product. These seem to be the most useful and thought out programs, without a lot of customizing, the square peg doesn't usually fit into the round hole.

Make sure the people you are speaking with can talk computer, or at least sound like they can. Continuing tech support is invaluable, especially to the small agency that may not have a full time computer person.

To finish up those spectacular tales of brave and daring, use a printer. Printers are getting smaller and smaller, they can fit into tiny places, and be removed when needed. They're not very expensive, usually around $50.00 and up. Lots of officers I work with have installed bubble jet type printers into their cars, so they can print reports, on the street and hand them directly to the supervisor, after they dry. Cords power these units that can be plugged into the cigarette lighter, if you can find yours.

Resources

Black's Law Dictionary, Henry Campbell Black

The Holt Handbook, Kirszner and Mandell

Photos courtesy of Florida Department of Law Enforcement

Index

Abbreviations 65
Absolutes 75
Affiant 86
Arrest Affidavits 79, 81
Arrests 70
  physical 81
Automated Law Enforcement Incident Report . . . 109
Capitals 65
Circumstantial 74
Circumstantial Evidence
  defined 74
Closure 52
Complainant 28
  determine who is 28
Computer Report Writing 105
Computers in the police car 106
Conclusions 74
Confrontation Continuum 93
Contractions 60
Control an interview 7
Crime scene 38
Crime Scene Log 21
Dates 26
Death investigation 77
Describing injuries 77
Dialogue 94
Environmental factors 93
Evidence
  chain of custody of 84

Exclamation point 63
Generic Arrest Affidavit 85, 87, 88
Generic Police Report . . . 31, 34, 36, 37, 39, 40, 43, 45, 47-50, 53
Grammar and Spelling 55
Heading 34, 47
Hearsay 61
How you received this call 35
Identification 52
Immediate actions taken by you 37
Intent 98
Interview 8, 45
Interview on tape 102
Investigation 33
Investigative actions 40
Letter style 26
Location 27
Narrative 33
Narrative style 33
Obtaining information 12
Officers 71
Officers' responsibilities 73
Organizing your thoughts 34
Page numbers 30
Parentheses 61
Perimeter search 43
Physical arrest 81
Physical evidence 19
Privacy and Legal Issues 67
Probable cause 84
Pronouns 64
Property 29
Prosecution 53
Punctuation 59
Question mark 63